HOSPITALITY

IN

HEALTHCARE

HOSPITALITY

— IN —

HEALTHCARE

How Top Performing Practices Boost
Team Happiness and Give the Best in
Care to Their Patients

Debbie Boone, CVPM

Published by Press 49, a division of BMH Companies LLC, Chandler, Arizona

This book is brought to you with the support of CareCredit® and Pets Best. Synchrony and its affiliates, including CareCredit® and Pets Best, share this information solely for your convenience. All statements are the sole opinions of the author, and Synchrony makes no representations or warranties regarding the content.

Some names have been changed to protect individuals' privacy.

Volume pricing is available to bulk orders placed by corporations, associations, and others. For bulk order details and for media inquiries, please contact Press 49 at info@press49.com or 833.PRESS49 (833.773.7749).

FIRST EDITION

Library of Congress Control Number: 2023908427
ISBN: 978-1-953315-30-4 (Hardcover)
ISBN: 978-1-953315-32-8 (Hardcover Special Edition)
ISBN: 978-1-953315-29-8 (eBook)

BUS070170 BUSINESS & ECONOMICS / Industries / Healthcare
REF004000 REFERENCE / Business Skills

Printed in the United States of America.

DEDICATION

This book is dedicated to my parents, Ralph and Mildred Huey, who believed in offering the best in hospitality to everyone who dined with them. Thankfully, they taught their children their "farm kid" work ethic, an uncompromising desire for quality, and true Southern hospitality.

Special thanks go to Dr. Steve Cobb who gave me my first job in a veterinary clinic and who taught me how to successfully run a practice.

To the many veterinary professionals, veterinary technicians, assistants and client service representatives I have had the pleasure to work beside and teach, your commitment to the animals in your care and their people inspire me daily.

Thank you also to all those in the profession who gave me so many wonderful opportunities to share my message.

To the multitude of animals that have shared my life, especially my dogs who show hospitality to friends and strangers alike with a wagging tail and a jump for joy greeting. We can learn a lot from them.

To my much-loved Football Girls and Hens—these women are my "sisters by choice." Everyone needs a posse, and you are mine.

To Brenda Andresen who took a casual conversation over coffee and turned it into a reality and to CareCredit's team who supported the idea, I am infinitely grateful.

Finally, to my husband, Mike, who is my rock through all of life's ups and downs. He encouraged me to take the big leap of starting my business. He supports my passion for my work by keeping my home life on track, and he keeps me centered. He is my sounding board, my cheerleader, my editor, and my in-house business guru. He makes me laugh every day. He has been the love of my life since we met in high school, and each year together just gets better. Growing old with you is my deepest desire.

Contents

Advance Praise
for Hospitality in Healthcare

"*Hospitality in Healthcare* gives veterinary clinics the keys to unlocking extraordinary experiences for veterinary clients. In this exceptional work, veterinary practice consultant Debbie Boone, CVPM reveals the transformative power of excellent customer service in the world of animal care.

With unrivaled expertise and a passion for both animals and their human companions, Debbie takes readers on a captivating journey, revealing the untapped potential within every veterinary hospital. Seamlessly blending practical strategies with heartwarming anecdotes, she demonstrates how a culture of hospitality can redefine the veterinary experience.

Through the pages of this enlightening book, you'll discover the profound impact of a warm smile, a comforting word, and a genuine connection with clients. Meticulous insights provide invaluable guidance on improving communication, cultivating empathy, and fostering trust—a recipe for creating and offering an exceptional environment where pets and their owners feel welcomed and cared for.

Hospitality in Healthcare is a testament to the importance of exceptional customer service in veterinary medicine, a must-read for veterinary professionals and animal lovers alike."

Dr. Ernie Ward
Author of "Creating the Veterinary Experience"
Author of "Creating the Veterinary Appointment"
Award-winning practice owner and veterinarian, impact entrepreneur, and business consultant

"Debbie has taken her extensive wisdom and accumulated knowledge shared with countless audiences over the years and put it all here for the veterinary world to benefit from. As one of the world's most respected voices in veterinary client care, Debbie's insights are sure to make the team stronger, the culture brighter, and the pet parents happier. Whether you're struggling to make a major shift or working near the top of your game and looking to take things to the next level, this book has gems for anyone looking to be just a little extra. A must-have for the discerning practice management bookshelf!"

Jessica Vogelsang, DVM
American Animal Hospital Association Chief Medical Officer
Author of *All Dogs Go To Kevin*

"Every time your team delivers veterinary medical care, the client is there (and returns) because of the experience. Sorry to burst your bubble, but their choice to return is rarely about the medicine. From the initial contact (whether on the phone or on your website) to conversations in the consult/exam room and the outcome, it's the hospitality received (or not) that bonds the client and their pet to your team and practice. In usual fashion, Debbie Boone, CVPM, does an eloquent job of supporting veterinary teams in communicating and creating an extraordinary experience. Take a deep dive with your team to learn more!"

Rebecca Rose, RVT
Certified Career Coach

"There's something truly special about the way Debbie opens up and shares her life experiences with vulnerability and clarity. It's a kind of honesty that's admirable and also incredibly valuable. There's an old saying that 'Clients don't care how much you know until they know how much you care.' Debbie perfectly communicates that sentiment in *Hospitality in Healthcare*.

She skillfully communicates essential workplace concepts like the importance of mattering, emotional intelligence, and psychological safety. Her storytelling and insightful observations really hit home.

Debbie focuses on creating a positive, memorable experience for our patients and clients. It's not just about providing a service; it's about making a difference. By doing this, she gives us powerful tools to enhance the meaning and purpose behind our work. I would recommend this read to any veterinary professional."

Philip Richmond, DVM, CAPP, CPHSA, CPPC, CCFP
Founder and CEO
Flourishing Phoenix Veterinary Consultants, LLC

"In businesses throughout every industry, success of any kind relies on the whims of people. The services and products we offer are less important than how we offer them. People who feel good in a purchase tend to repeat that purchase. With her distinctly unique voice, amplified by her expansive knowledge and thoughtful approach, Debbie Boone has given us a gift in *Hospitality in Healthcare* that provides us approachable tools to transform the client experience in our practices. Her approach to hospitality won't just benefit clients; it will elevate the care we're able to provide the patients we serve and, in turn, improve the wellbeing of the people of veterinary medicine. By the last page, you'll be inspired not only to serve your whole community better but by the natural hospitality that oozes from Debbie's words."

Josh Vaisman, MAPPCP
Founder and Lead Positive Change Agent
Flourish Veterinary Consulting

"Southern charm meets the business of veterinary medicine. Debbie shares how to make clients feel welcome, important, and respected. As a result, team members are happier, clients become fans, pets live longer, and the bottom line thrives."

Bob Lester, DVM
Co-founder and Chief Medical Officer
WellHaven Pet Health

"Veterinary medicine is a service industry that provides healthcare!! You may not like this statement, but you better get used to it. Our clients are having higher and higher expectations and we are delivering lower and lower value and service. The place to start in a service business is ... SERVICE. Client service!! Why not look to other industries to learn from? The hospitality industry survives on service. Debbie Boone has taken her knowledge and experiences as a consumer and combined them with her knowledge of the veterinary profession to create a tome that will lead your practice from being doctor-centric to being client savvy. Long term success in veterinary medicine requires putting the client (and patient) first and by emulating successes from other client-focused industries, and as Debbie demonstrates, you can do that."

Peter Weinstein, DVM, MBA
PAW Consulting
Simple Solutions 4 Vets, Inc.

"There are lots of social media tricks of the trade these days, but as Debbie Boone points out, the oldest and most persuasive PR remains the same as it's been forever, and that's word of mouth. While providing excellence in veterinary medical care is clearly important, even more significant is the way in which the entire staff makes clients and their pets feel. Customer care is more than a phrase; it's about empathetic action, demonstrating that each and every person in the practice truly cares about their clients and their patients. And when clients feel that you sincerely care, they will return for life and likely tell their friends and family. There's no real trick here, as Debbie points out in *Hospitality in Healthcare*; try to put yourself in the client's shoes and never think "it's us versus them.""

Steve Dale, CABC
Program host, WGN Radio and national radio programs
Speaker at veterinary meetings around the world
www.stevedale.tv

Introduction

The goal of this book is to revolutionize the lives of patients, clients, medical care professionals, and these professionals' teams by sharing how lessons and skills learned from the hospitality industry can transform the pre-visit, visit, and post-visit experience for all the participants.

I acknowledge that this is a bold statement, but having lived a life of providing hospitality to others, it is also something I know, from firsthand experience, that it works. It worked for the restaurants I grew up in and for the fabric shop and veterinary practices I managed. It works for the practices with which I consult. It will work for you, too. Every weekend, the restaurants had lines of patrons waiting to be seated, and even though it has been more than fifteen years since the last one closed, people still remember them and speak fondly of the food, the service, and the memories created. The fabric shop thrived on a loyal customer base and was one of the most prosperous in the chain. Using the skills of hospitality in a medical environment built our veterinary practices to be the most successful in our area. Our reputation in the community was stellar. We retained our team members for years, saw loyal clients whose kids then became loyal clients, our staff enjoyed their work, drama and client complaints were almost nonexistent, and we had a compliance rate on preventive care that was 30 points above the national benchmarks. The team was well compensated, and profits were at the high end of the industry standard. Other local practice owners wondered what the "magic formula" was that made our practice so unusual. It was hospitality!

Anyone who ever hears me speak instantly knows I am from the South. Born and raised in North Carolina, I was taught Southern hospitality from birth. Add to that the fact that my parents were successful restaurateurs who believed in teaching their kids to meet and serve the public from a young age, and you have the formula for my belief that learning to anticipate, personalize, and observe people's needs is the key to a happy team and a happy life. How do I know the employees were happy? Because they stayed even in tough times.

In 1973, my father committed suicide. He was a well-loved and well-respected person in our community, and everyone was shocked at his death. My mother was a thirty-nine-year-old widow with two teenagers to raise and multiple restaurants to manage. A few days after the funeral, my mom held a staff meeting and laid it all on the table to her employees. She needed their help to keep the business going, and she needed their expertise. Every single person stayed and pulled together to keep the business running without my father, and within a brief period of time, it was flourishing as never before.

As a child, I would observe the waitstaff find their "regulars" waiting in line to be seated. They would hurry to clear a table, get them seated, and serve those customers their usual beverages without them even having to ask. They remembered what the guests usually ate, confirmed their choices, reminded them when the special cobbler they liked was going to be on the menu and watched unobtrusively for a cue that the coffee needed a refill or when the plates were ready to be removed. They chatted and joked with those who enjoyed interaction or discreetly served those who preferred a quiet meal. This level of customer care extended into the kitchen where the cooks also knew the customers' preferences and cooked the fish a little browner or the steak a little rarer for certain folks. They would even prepare and slice homegrown tomatoes that some of the before-work regular breakfast crowd would bring to share with their revolving group of business buddies at our largest table in the front of the dining room. This was beyond ordinary service, but in our restaurant, it was the norm. That is why every Sunday after church let out, the lines to get in would often wrap around the building. Great service paired with great products is worth the wait.

In today's world, people are rarely served well. We go through our days with silent, unsmiling people shoving bags out a drive-through window at us, being ignored by retail workers who are afraid we may ask them a question, and being talked at by medical professionals who are speaking jargon and using terminology we don't understand. Then those same ineffective and discourteous workers wonder why the public is being so difficult. In retaliation, these inattentive employees spend their time complaining about the rude customers and non-compliant patients with whom they are forced to interact, sometimes even to the point of firing them as clients rather than taking any ownership in their part of the communication breakdown.

Hospitality changes all that.

Will some customers be challenging? Of course. You will always serve someone who is having a difficulty you know nothing about, yet they bring that to your table. But utilizing superior communication skills, having emotional self-control, and diagnosing how to resolve a challenge can turn that "grump" into a fan. The result? A better workplace where clients trust you, listen to your recommendations, and become avid supporters for years to come. When this happens, coming to work becomes enjoyable, *especially when we use the same hospitality skills to care for each other.*

Hospitality is not just "being nice." People who are not naturally nice can still be hospitable, and extremely nice folks can still serve poorly. Hospitality is a mindset and a skill. This book is a guide into developing this mindset for your own wellbeing and the success of the business you own or in which you work. Hospitality can also help in your personal life as the skills learned work on all humans and not just customers, clients, or patients.

I hope you enjoy the book as I share the lessons learned from a lifetime of joyfully and successfully serving others.

Debbie Boone, CVPM

1

Know Your Purpose

It may seem odd to begin a book on hospitality with a chapter on purpose, however, humans are put on earth to accomplish things. We evolved as part of a tribe that collaborated to undertake tasks that allowed us to survive. If we worked together sharing our individual skills, we thrived. Alone, we died. *Purpose* in Neanderthal days was simple. Food, water, reproduction, and safety were the goals. As man evolved, our goals became more elaborate. Humans still desire to eat and drink, but now it may be a sumptuous dish from a top chef and well-crafted wine from a five-star restaurant. We certainly want to feel safe physically, but also mentally. Much of good hospitality focuses on creating psychological safety for those we serve. Similar to animals, most bad behavior by humans is based in fear. Hospitality allows fear to subside and trust to thrive.

Simon Sinek is best known for shining light on the importance of knowing our purpose. His explanation of the Golden Circles in *Start With Why: How Great Leaders Inspire Everyone to Take Action* is one of my favorite tools to share when training. He says most people define themselves by "what" they do, then advertise "how" they do it when instead they should start with "why" they do things, then move outward to what they do and how they do it. WHY matters to our soul and keeps us focused, especially when the "how" part gets difficult.

As someone who has spent more than thirty-five years in veterinary medicine, I can attest that it is a purpose-driven profession. Yet, when asked "What do you do?" those same animal health advocates will say "I am a doctor" or "I am a technician" when what they really do is partner with pet owners to help provide a healthy life for their patients with preventive care and owner education and to save animal lives in times of crises. That is BIG! Too much emphasis is placed on *what* we do over *why* we do it. Focusing on the *task* of our work diminishes the higher purpose of our jobs. The medical field, whether animal or human, requires hours of rigorous education, training, and developing proficiency of task. But when we lose sight of the true reason for performing those tasks, they become a burden to be borne rather than the means to a higher end.

Over the years, I have observed team members go above and beyond the call of duty in volunteer jobs. My veterinary assistants and technicians carried neonatal kittens home to bottle feed them every couple of hours day and night. They fostered unwanted animals and worked a network of connections to find them good homes. All this work was done without pay, on their own time, and with the only reward being the satisfaction of helping those animals.

Purpose surpasses money in the human psyche.

This is not to say that appropriate pay is not important, but choosing work that satisfies the soul and allows us to pay our bills is far superior to a job that we feel is "just working for a paycheck." That type of job is usually reflected in our attitude towards it. Dread overtakes joy, and we grind away doing the minimum we can to avoid getting fired.

When we work for purpose, we make the effort to go beyond the job description. Rather we take that base and build on it to create an experience for those we serve that is memorable, positive, and connected.

> **It is the duty of the leaders of any business to define the higher purpose of the work, hire people who desire to demonstrate that purpose, and put systems in place that allow them to accomplish their goals of doing good in the world.**

You can always tell when an employee enjoys their job. Their attitude is engaged in performing their tasks with excellence and creativity. They connect with the patient, client, customer, and fellow staff members in a genuine and caring manner. They also flourish in environments where extra effort, positive attitude, and genuine commitment are acknowledged and rewarded. Even the most purpose-filled employee can be ruined by a poor leader. If this occurs, you will find these workers leave for better cultures, or they wither away to become below average or, on occasion, even toxic employees.

Serving the public is not always easy. People can be difficult, unreasonable, and even frightening. Knowing that serving them well and having the skills to overcome all those negatives can lead to accomplishing your purpose and makes the discomfort more tolerable. Sometimes conquering the ornery customer makes us feel more victorious than when we serve the easy ones. It is in those situations we get to show off our hospitality talents and think, "Damn! I am good!" We give ourselves a mental high five when that cranky patron leaves with a smile. Surprisingly, those well-managed grumps can turn into some of your most loyal fans.

Learning hospitality skills can help us accomplish the aspirations of our work, which go beyond getting a paycheck. When we achieve our goals, we feel better about our lives, and even on difficult days filled with challenging cases and demanding humans, we can walk out the door and feel we made a positive mark on the world.

EXERCISE: Consider what your personal purpose is at work. Does it align with the business purpose? If not, what can you do to become more aligned?

2

Know Your Brand

Several years ago, I consulted with a veterinary practice in Pennsylvania. This was a highly successful five-doctor hospital, but they were having some issues. As I interviewed the doctors and staff, I discovered an inconsistency between the practice owners and the team regarding the position of the hospital in the community. The practice was accredited by the American Animal Hospital Association (AAHA), and it practiced to a high standard of care. The facility itself was slightly dated but immaculately clean and uncluttered. There was a combination of longtime employees and several fairly new ones. After interviewing the staff, I felt like many of the newer employees did not understand the practice's origin story nor did they have a strong belief in the brand of the practice and how it was different from others in the town.

Branding is a marketing term. According to Oberlo, a Shopify platform, "Branding is the process of creating a strong, positive perception of your company, and its products in your customer's mind." This statement is accurate; however, it leaves out an important aspect of branding, which is the employees must also have a strong positive perception of the company and be engaged in the creation of a superb customer experience. Every business has a story to tell, and the team should all know and appreciate the story. They must feel like what they offer the patrons they serve is unique and special. If it can be done with coffee, it certainly can be done in medicine.

International best-selling author and keynote speaker, Kindra Hall has made a name for herself by telling stories and helping businesses discover and fine tune their brand story. In her book, *Choose Your Story, Change Your Life: Silence Your Inner Critic and Rewrite Your Life from the Inside Out,* she offers a list of questions to help people recall important moments that bring out the real narrative behind the company. My favorite is "Whose life is different because of your business?" What an amazing reflection about the effect our most routine efforts make in the lives of others.

As I began my training session with the Pennsylvania practice, I asked them, "What is your favorite memory of a moment in practice?" **Two stories stood out.**

The first. One of the senior veterinary technicians recalled the time she got to help treat a bald eagle. She said the grandeur and magnificence of this bird was breathtaking. Her heart started to race just from its presence. The very fact that she got the opportunity to touch this incredible animal and help it back into the sky was a moment that she would remember the rest of her life. You could see the memory come back to her and the power of working to save the bird made her remember the reason for all her education and training.

The second. The practice owner was on call for after-hours emergencies when he received a page. One of the local canine officers had been hurt protecting his handler during an arrest and was gravely wounded. The doctor rushed to the practice, calling for his support team to meet him there. All worked frantically to save the dog, but unfortunately, the damage was too severe and the patient was lost. Except the memory wasn't really about the dog but rather about the community of fellow officers who appeared at the hospital to support their canine comrade during his surgery. When they were made aware of the death of their comrade, they ordered appropriate transportation for the body, then all the officers followed their fallen canine teammate in a police honor guard as he was driven to his final resting place. The practice owner said, "It was then I saw the impact of the human-animal bond. Even for these tough law enforcement officers who saw the worst of humanity on a daily basis, that dog was more than a working tool—he was a companion and respected ally, and they honored him as such. I felt the importance and impact of my work on that night."

Both stories helped clarify the purpose behind the work. As we continued the meeting, other staff members told stories of helping animals and humans and the feelings behind the reactions they received. They were able to define their brand story as a company that was there in times of need for two- and four-legged creatures, all while acknowledging the value of their services to sustain the joy and importance of those human-animal bonds. They realized that it was because of their AAHA accreditation, the superior medical care, years of experience, and modern equipment they boasted that these opportunities came to them. So, the brand became about progressive medicine leading to exceptional opportunities to help in unique situations. They were special because they were prepared for the routine as well as the uncommon.

EXERCISE: Recall a moment in your work that is your favorite memory. Did it help identify your purpose?

Once you clarify your brand, you begin to look for ways to exhibit it to the community. We all understand the difference between Walmart and Nordstrom. They each serve a different customer population, and as such, they set up their stores in ways that are appropriate to a targeted demographic. Walmart focuses on low price and carries everything from clothing to cleaning supplies. Customers go to Walmart for bargains. Nordstrom focuses on higher quality merchandise for a shopper who values and can afford designer brands and who seeks top-quality materials and garment construction. Nordstrom is also known for superior customer service, which is a match for its brand. Walmart shoppers generally do not expect to have clothing selections carried to a dressing room for them and personal attention given as they try on outfits. Nordstrom customers do.

Obviously, hospitality plays a part in both experiences. The question being posed by all consumers is "How will I be served?" Customers visiting a bargain-branded business usually have lower experience expectations than those visiting more expensive ones. Therefore, giving a better-than-expected experience in a low-priced store is usually easy and a delightful surprise to the customer. Case in point—there was a Goodwill store near my former home, and the bookworm in me frequented it often, searching for bargain business books. The staff members were always friendly and helpful with pleasant greetings for every customer. Even Goodwill can show hospitality.

We have all been through the fast-food drive-through window and had our order taken by a person who attempts to rush us through our selections, mumbles a price total over the microphone, and tells us to drive up to the next window. When we arrive and pay, a bag is handed over with a scripted but meaningless *"thank you,"* and we only hope the food order is correct and that maybe we have a few napkins. Then there is the Chick-fil-A experience. Some protest their religious policies, but no one can dispute they are the outstanding customer service title holders of fast food. In his book, *How Did You Do it Truett?: A Recipe for Success,"* Truett Cathy, the founder of Chick-fil-A, said it was about "creating a culture that sets, expects, and rewards high standards and performance." Every business should follow this advice and build this type of culture. One of Truett's long-time employees, Zelma Calhoun, worked for him for forty-five years. When asked what made her so loyal, she said, "I've never heard Mr. Cathy raise his voice. I don't remember him arguing with anybody. I've never heard him tell somebody to do something. He would ask ...."

> **It's about creating a culture that sets, expects, and rewards high standards and performance.**

In today's high turnover employee market, perhaps leaders should follow Mr. Cathy's lead. It certainly seemed to work. Truett Cathy understood hospitality and used it for customers and his team. If we expect our staff to serve our clients to high standards, we must remember that leaders model the behaviors that are acceptable for everyone who works there. If snide remarks and shouting at each other are allowed within the ranks, expect no better behavior when those same employees are facing your clients. As the old saying goes, "Shit rolls downhill!"

Other companies have strong brand recognition. Starbucks has the green mermaid, but they also write the customer's name on each cup of coffee so that they soon come to learn their regulars. Target has a brand known for reasonable pricing yet unique design not to mention the bright white of the floors and walls accented by big red targets that make us feel we are in a well-organized, immaculately clean space. My husband loves to visit Bass Pro Shops. Their buildings house areas for camping, hunting, and fishing with their well-known aquarium filled with multiple kinds of fish at center stage. When you enter Bass Pro Shops, you expect and see lodge pole beams, flannel shirts, fishing poles, and camping stoves. They don't sell silk pajamas as that would be off brand. Their staff are hired for their knowledge of outdoor sports, and they offer guidance when customers are purchasing goods. Being outdoorsy is their brand.

What do your clients picture when they think of your business? For a veterinary office or a medical or dental office, the first impression should be "immaculate cleanliness" with only pleasant odors detectable. Smell is a powerful trigger of memory and emotion for animals and humans alike. Animals react to them at the veterinary practice if they trigger memories of discomfort and will balk at the door. As a breast cancer survivor, I recall fanatically washing my hands during the months of my chemo treatments. The Cancer Center at Duke had a very particular handwash in the bathrooms called Steris. It had a medical smell, and twenty years later, if I smell it, I get a nauseating grab in my gut because it brings me into that chemotherapy room once again.

As the hospital administrator of a top tier veterinary practice, I made sure that the facility was clean and smelled pleasant when clients walked in the door. The staff were well-dressed, and the parking lot was maintained without potholes and was freshly striped on a regular basis. One small touch that also stayed on-brand were our magazines. Everyone has been to the doctor's office that offers dog eared five-year-old *People* and *Time* magazines. I made sure that was never the case in our practice. Our magazines reflected the interests of our clients. *Veranda*, *Southern Living*, *Architectural Digest*, *Vogue*, *Time*, *Reader's Digest,* and *Newsweek* were all fresh and on the wall rack. One of our clients even took the time to find the practice owner and comment, "You always have the BEST magazines." Though it seems insignificant, those magazines made a statement about our brand. If a client was really enjoying a magazine, we would offer to gift it to them. If you are a veterinary office, don't make the mistake of having only animal magazines in your lobby. Your clients have pets, but they have many additional interests so provide variety in your selection.

The devil really is in the details when shaping your brand and the customer experience that accompanies it, those subtle nuances matter more than you know.

EXERCISE: What small touches or fine details help define your office brand? What could you add to make your brand stand out from the crowd?

3

Clients Want an Experience, Not Just an Appointment

Every time we walk into the door of a business, we receive an experience. On occasion, the experience is negative. For the most part, our experiences are nondescript. They're not particularly good nor are they particularly bad. They leave us with no emotional response at all. It's unfortunate that the majority of our experiences are like this. Except on occasion, we encounter someone who completely transforms our standard experience and leaves us with a smile on our face and a glowing opinion of the company for which they work. Because we are so accustomed to mediocre service, small improvements can make big impressions.

One of the biggest complaints in both veterinary and human medicine is wait time. As a patient, my longest wait time beyond my scheduled appointment was two hours. Because I was waiting for one of the top oncologists in the United States, I was willing to accept the delay, but if I had been waiting for my dental hygienist I certainly would have rescheduled or found another provider.

Medical care providers tend to forget that they must provide a positive experience for their client or patient. In fact, it was the poor customer service experience I had with the first oncologist I visited after my breast cancer diagnosis that ended up costing that hospital more than a million dollars in lost revenue. More on how I arrived at that figure later.

In truth, my experience with my cancer diagnosis had multiple hospitality flaws. I had noticed a lump on my breast and because of a history of cysts, I casually visited my friend's plastic surgery practice to have it checked. She immediately became alarmed when she was unable to draw fluid from the lump and sent me to a well-respected local radiologist. She happened to be out of the office that day, so I saw her associate.

I was prepared for a mammogram then an ultrasound, and as I lay there on the table wondering if I had cancer, this doctor and her assistant stood above me and talked about an imminent visit from the doctor's in-laws and the stress that she was under. At first, I was certain they would quickly finish their personal conversation and concentrate on me. But that never happened. I laid there feeling like an inanimate object, secondary in their focus. There was no attempt to connect with me. Empathy was never shared. I was a "chore" to be performed and quickly sent out the door so as to not bother the doctor who had other more important things to think about. I felt like an unwelcome distraction rather than a valuable patient whose health mattered.

The ultrasound was inconclusive, so I was sent away to return in three weeks. Once again, the ultrasound was unable to be read, and once again, I was to return. Finally, on the third trip, the mass was biopsied, and when I returned a week later for the results, a different doctor was there. I remember distinctly being called into the x-ray room and seated on a rolling backless stool and having a stranger I had never seen say, "I am sorry, Mrs. Boone, but you have breast cancer." I couldn't believe that a conversation this important and heavy was to be conducted in a working area full of equipment rather than while seated in a private location. This was life-changing news, and it deserved a better plan for delivery. Because of my familiarity with medicine, I quickly asked, "What kind?" This doctor gave me a bewildered look and answered with "the normal kind." I asked to see my pathology report.

Most women know that there is not a "normal" kind of cancer, especially when it is your cancer. Some types are certainly more common, but others are aggressive and difficult to treat. There are plenty of television commercials to teach us those facts. We all have someone in our circle who has been through cancer treatment, so we know enough to recognize bad news from *really bad news*. Some assurance that mine was a non-aggressive type would have definitely eased some of my fear as it would for anyone in my shoes. Needless to say, I was less than impressed with this entire event because it not only made me feel uncared for, but it also made me question the competence of the group. In an appropriate scenario, with concern for my feelings, I would have been taken to a doctor's office with the door shut, spoken with someone I had actually seen before, given an empathetic statement by the doctor who could have said, "I am sorry to share that you have cancer, however, it is adenocarcinoma, which is the most common type of breast cancer and usually successfully treated." I know I could have found some relief and hope in that statement as would anyone in my circumstances.

My next visit was to a surgeon whom I knew from a previous surgery. It was at his office that I felt the first true empathy on this terrible journey. After hearing his advice, my husband and I moved on to see the recommended oncologist. This doctor had stellar credentials having formerly been on the transplant team at Duke. However, after a brief visit where he looked at my chart—rarely at me—offered a plan without my input, and seemed completely unconcerned about the possible outcome of my treatment, I left.

My husband looked at me as we crossed the parking lot and said, "This man will not be your doctor because to him you are not a person—only a chart."

And that is exactly what I felt like. I was a medical problem to be solved, not a human who was starting a fight for her life and who needed an ally and a guide.

Thanks to serendipity, connections, and a few phone calls, I became a patient at Duke University Cancer Center. My experience with this group was 180 degrees different. I was fortunate that I had the opportunity to have this world-class hospital just forty miles from my home not only because of the exceptional medical skill residing within its walls but because of the equally excellent hospitality of my medical care team. I particularly remember one of the receptionists in the oncology clinic who treated every patient like she truly cared about them. As nerve-racking as those visits were, she was always kind and engaged. It's been twenty years, and I still remember her. And I still return to Duke once a year for routine mammograms and exams, driving four hours from North Myrtle Beach, South Carolina to Durham, North Carolina because I trust them so deeply.

My good friend, Pamela, and I are both cancer survivors who were treated at Duke. We started a breast cancer survivor group at our very large church. As women came into the group, we advised them to have treatment at the Duke Cancer Center rather than at the local hospital, and I certainly steered them away from the oncologist I first encountered. Over the next few years, I personally sent at least fifteen other women to my doctors and to the Duke facility. Pamela did the same. By the time my treatment was finished, my hospital bills totaled more than $150,000. And if you calculated each of the referral's treatment at only $100,000, you can see how my single, less-than-stellar patient experience ended up costing the original hospital in excess of a million dollars in lost revenue.

Like a stone falling into a pool of water, the ripples of my positive service experience moved outward to create a patient referral group of my making, and we can most certainly add to the tally the patients that those women referred after they got an equally excellent experience. The repercussions are infinite.

What could those initial providers have done to make my experience better?

First, the radiologist could have recognized that the most stressed person in the room was me, not her, regardless of *anything* she may have had going on in her life. My visit should have never been about her anxiety about a visit from her in-laws. It should have been a time where my concerns were addressed and details given about the need for my return, and upon the second visit, action should have been proactively taken to biopsy the lump. She delayed almost another month because she assumed my friend's attempt to aspirate the mass created blood in the area. Yes, she threw her under the bus with this assumption—a whole other issue. Second, it appeared the uncomfortable conversation with me about my positive diagnosis had been pawned off on the intern who was obviously poorly or inadequately trained to hold it. My diagnosis was given to me in a room with little privacy while sitting on an uncomfortable rolling stool in an x-ray room. If I had broken down into tears, I don't think there was even a box of tissues available. When a patient asks an obviously informed question like I did when I asked the type of cancer, it should register with the provider that they are working with a person with some degree of medical knowledge. The conversation should then be tailored to their level. Offices ask patients and clients to fill out forms that ask where they work or their profession. Providers should use this information to tailor how they speak with the people they serve, conversing in terms and on levels that are equally respectful to and informative for the patient.

What about the first oncologist? He could have changed his greeting from the typical handshake and generic "*Nice to meet you*" to something more in alignment with the gravity of the situation. Perhaps saying "*I know this is frightening and I am here to help*" would have been more appropriate before he flipped through the two pages in my brand-new chart in order to avoid eye contact with me. This was a person that I could have spent many hours with while going through treatment. As a patient, I wanted someone by my side who cared about me as a human.

Conversely, when I went to Duke and met my oncologist, he spoke with me and my husband about what this journey would look like for both of us. He understood how stressful it was and even allowed me to record our initial conversation so I could play it back when I got home. He took my hand, touched my forearm, and looked me in the eyes with great empathy. That was when I knew I had found the team that would save my life.

Understand that the experience is not limited to interactions with the doctors but encompasses the entire staff. An impatient remark by the person answering the phone can begin a downward spiral that continues into the facility visit. Often a poor encounter on the phone when attempting to simply schedule an appointment can lead that potential client to change their mind or merely be a "no show" for their scheduled time because they called another provider and got a friendly voice and a genuine connection.

Poor experiences also occur when there's a lack of follow-through and consistency. On a recent annual visit to my general practitioner, my bloodwork showed an elevated A1C. The doctor wanted to repeat the test in three months. I scheduled the lab appointment for three months later and returned as planned. However, when my test results came back, my A1C test was not listed in the results. Upon calling back to find out why, I was told not to be concerned, that it wasn't high enough to matter. You can see there was an inconsistency between what the doctor told me in the exam room the day she reported it was elevated and what I was told three months later over the phone after returning for additional testing at her request. Did she really not mean to order the test, or did someone drop the ball and then tell me it was unimportant just to cover up a mistake? This confusion has me questioning whether I need to search for a new doctor.

When I managed veterinary hospitals, hospitality was one of our major focuses. If you bought a bag of food, there was a likelihood the practice owner would carry it to the car for you and if not him, certainly one of the staff members. Even over client protests, this small courtesy was performed. Clients' names were remembered as were their kids' and pets' names and were used in conversation. Connections were made whether it was a comment about a cute pair of shoes they were wearing or the novel they had in hand. Our team observed our clients and found ways to build relationships. Those relationships kept our clients loyal and formed a referral network for us beyond what any paid advertisement or marketing plan could possibly provide. Client retention was high and often multi-generational. Understand that this practice was in a large city, not a small town. We just gave folks that small town feeling and showed them that they mattered regardless of the size of the city or the practice.

One day, one of our former competitors attended my class on customer service. He was the regional medical director for a large corporate practice group. At the break, he came up to me and said, "Debbie, every veterinarian in town wanted to know what the hell you people were doing at that practice. I used to get some of your boarding overflow during the holidays, and try as we might, even though we were less expensive, we could not get those people to change to us. Now I understand that it wasn't the medicine but the hospitality that keep those clients so loyal."

I just smiled.

There are a lot of wonderful veterinarians and doctors out there, but since clients are not usually medical professionals, they make judgments based only on how they feel when visiting the office. We worked to make clients feel welcome, important, and respected. The team was also well-trained, and systems were in place to make sure things like my A1C snafu didn't happen. This positive energy was returned to us in trust, compliance, and referrals. Since we measured where all our new clients came from, we knew that well over 80 percent came from referrals from our existing clients.

Care for your health or for your pet's health is an emotional event. Just consider how someone's blood pressure will rise simply from the sight of a white coat at a doctor visit. For animals, they smell the odors of the hospital and pheromones of other fearful pets and become reluctant to enter the door. When we consider the emotions at play in a trip to the practice and train our team on how to influence them in a positive way, it is a win for all stakeholders.

The real payoff when clients and patients have a great experience is the wellbeing of the team. Happy people don't get angry and upset and give employees a hard time. Animals who are not fearful because staff acknowledge their fear and overcome it with treats and low-stress handling better tolerate and even like their veterinary visits. This makes everyone's job easier and much more enjoyable. When trust is built and maintained with those we serve, they become more amenable to our offerings and directives. "Yes" becomes the norm as opposed to "You only care about the money" or "You are in bed with the drug company and get kickbacks." I always laugh when I hear this because the rules are so stringent—pharma reps can't even give away ink pens without scrutiny, and veterinarians certainly don't get big bonuses from pet food manufacturers. I know because I see their books.

I once received a call from one of my favorite practice managers. She asked me to help with some team training because she said, "Our team is spiraling into negativity and the client has now become our ENEMY." I was seeing the same murmurs online. Acknowledge that this is happening in your practice and address it expediently and appropriately.

Recognize that the pandemic exacerbated this poor behavior, but social unrest, politics, too much time disconnected from others, and social media echo chambers are all damaging the fabric of our humanity. Dehumanization of others causes otherwise normally kind and ethical people to go against their core beliefs. As an example, the Nazis called Jews "vermin and rats." Slaveholders justified their acceptance of slavery by stating that those they enslaved were "subhuman." Native Americans were deemed "savages" in order to feel no remorse in stealing native lands. So, when we dehumanize our clients by calling them "idiots, assholes, or fools," we are doing the same thing, and if allowed to continue, it will poison our business, our culture, and our very souls.

For now, just being aware of how client bashing is damaging our own mental health is a strong incentive to change. Negativity is an energy suck. Neuroscience research studies show that our brain seeks what we tell it to find. So, if we look for negative things, we will find them and dwell on them to our own detriment. That is why mindfulness and gratitude are so valuable in retraining our brain to seek the positive.

As a service industry, team members can never forget that clients are the source of our livelihood. They are the decision-makers for the pet that we want to treat. They also have a lot of choices where to spend their money. There were five good quality practices within a two-mile radius of my first practice, so I grew up in veterinary medicine dealing with a lot of competition. To top it all, our practice was probably the most expensive in town and one of the most successful because of the bond we built with our clients and each other.

During the COVID-19 pandemic, clients became a faceless voice–often a rude one. We missed out on the chit-chat, small talk, and personal encounters that make us human to each other. Now when our conversations are all limited to business and medical transactions, we are missing something vital for our clients and ourselves—connection with others.

How do we regain connection?

Communication training can help people understand their own reactions and those of their clients. When we have emotional intelligence, we can more easily navigate the choppy waters of human anxiety and stress. This goes for your external customer–the client—and your internal customer–the staff. Treat them both with kindness and empathy and support their goals; and trust me–life will improve for everyone. When you treat people well, gain their trust, and build a base of raving fans, your business will be successful and a wonderful place to work.

> **EXERCISE:** Reflect on a medical visit for you or your pet. Did you feel the providers cared about you as a person? How did they show you they cared? Or did you experience lack of caring? What could have been improved?

4

The Story: Who is the Hero? (Hint ... It's Not You)

Being from the South, I think I was born to be a storyteller. My father's side of the family was particularly good at spinning a yarn and certainly fabricating a tall tale. Still, true stories are always the best to share when moving people to action. Stories are powerful, especially in business. I mentioned earlier the value of storytelling in sharing your purpose and understanding your brand. But stories can go much further. They make training engaging and dramatically improve retention. They help people visualize and express goals and dreams. They can be used as cautionary tales of what not to do. They can inspire us to do things beyond our comfort zone. They can make us see others as more human when we walk in their shoes through their story.

In the book *Building a Story Brand: Clarify Your Message So Customers Will Listen* by Donald Miller, Miller does an exceptional job showing his reader how to define and create the story of their customer's journey. As an avid reader, I have whiled away many hours engrossed in a good book. I identify with the heroine, aspire to be the wizard who knows all, and embrace the joy of a happy ending by living vicariously through the characters. According to Miller, this framework is required for any successful novel, movie, or play. We must always have the main character who is our hero. They must be faced with some sort of challenge that they cannot solve on their own. Along comes the wise counselor (think Merlin from *Tales of King Arthur*) who guides them along the path. The storyline continues with the hero moving through the quest or journey and the wise counselor guiding them along the way. Problems are solved and decisions are made. The goal is resolution of the challenge resulting in a positive outcome. The end. When the final outcome is negative and the hero loses, we are dissatisfied and don't care for the story.

In medicine, a mistake is often made in identifying the hero. Doctors regularly go into medicine with the idea that they will be saviors of their patients and gain adulation from them or, in veterinary medicine, from their patient's owner. Consequently, the storyline in those practices revolves around the practitioner. The websites and marketing content tell stories about the doctor's accomplishments, degrees, and awards. In veterinary medicine, the animal is often deemed the hero. Patients and clients are inconvenienced to accommodate the whim of the practitioner. Inadequate appointment times are allocated because time management overrides the needs of the customer. Practices chronically run behind, making clients wait. Arrogance replaces respect.

I once performed some consulting in a veterinary teaching hospital. On the day of my visit, multiple complex surgical cases had been scheduled. The evening before, several of the veterinary specialists who were scheduled to perform these surgeries decided, without notice to their boss or team, to go to a conference a couple of hours away. This caused their patient care coordinators to have to call the pet owners, apologize for the late notice, cancel the surgeries, and attempt to reschedule them. These doctors gave absolutely no consideration to the anxiety or stress of the pet owners who had already mentally, physically, and logistically prepared to bring their pet to the specialty hospital. It is likely that the clients had asked to be off work, had to arrange childcare, or make some other kind of plan to enable them to transport their ailing pet to the hospital. No consideration was given to fellow team members such as the patient care coordinators who were on the frontline with the clients. They had to make those calls; finagle the surgical schedule; and field the irritation and, quite likely, the wrath of these disrespected pet owners. In this scenario, it is obvious that these doctors considered themselves to be the hero. Their own self-interest and self-importance led their decision-making. Because they were tenured, the employer had little recourse to reprimand this selfish behavior. I'm sure you are thinking, *"That would never happen in my practice."* But sometimes the slights are not as egregious as in this story, but they are still present. For instance, when service providers schedule appointments for 8 a.m. and show up to work at 8:30, causing patients to have a longer wait before they are seen, the same self-centered mentality is manifested. Thoughts of "self" have superseded respect for others.

Wise counselors are there for the heroes. They support, guide, and coach with empathy, respect, and knowledge. They desire the hero to win, and they offer their skills to make that happen. That is not to say the councilors should not set boundaries. They should. Even wizards take a break to rest, study their craft, and renew their powers.

> **"The purpose of life is not to be happy. It is to be useful, to be honorable, to be compassionate, to have it make some difference that you have lived and lived well."**
>
> —Ralph Waldo Emerson

When we focus on hospitality, we realize the medical team's position is to be the educator and knowledgeable guide to solving the hero's problem, which can be their own illness or an issue with their pet. When we realize our focus needs to shift, then our communication manner will change from authoritarian dictator to empathetic collaborator. If we want to live a life with purpose and accomplishment, we must focus on serving others well. Never being subservient but instead being helpful, empathic, and giving others grace when they are not at their best. The goal is to look back on your day and know you left the world a little better than you found it.

EXERCISE: Review your company website, social media posts, and internal focus. Who is front and center? Is it the client, or is it the medical staff? How would you edit the "story" so it is properly focused on the real "hero"?

5

Appearance and First Impressions

I have a photograph from my family's archives of the opening of our first restaurant. The waitresses were all dressed in white starched uniforms with white nurse's shoes. The kitchen staff wore white chef's coats, black pants, and white aprons. The equipment in the photograph gleamed. Everything about this picture spoke of cleanliness, quality, and attention to detail. Over the years, the business grew and the uniforms changed, but the attention to detail, cleanliness, and quality never wavered.

We certainly live in a more relaxed society when it comes to clothing than we did in the 1950s. Nevertheless, first impressions still matter.

Neuroscience teaches us that our brain is an energy hog, and therefore, it creates shortcuts in order to conserve calories. One of those shortcuts is snap judgments. Accurate or not, the instant we meet a new person our brain and our biases go to work to quickly place them in a category we understand. We are judging the person in front of us as someone we can trust or distrust. We determine if they are competent. Maybe they look like someone we didn't care for, and we transfer that dislike over to a stranger. Perhaps they make a remark that goes against our beliefs, and we never give them an opportunity to show us their entire self. The brain likes to "sort." The problem is many times our brain is dead wrong!

Not only are we judging the people in front of us, but we are also judging their surroundings. If there is clutter, we assume they are disorganized.

If their area is too Spartan, we assume they are too rigid. We look at hair, makeup, hands, nails, shoes, clothing, jewelry, cars, homes, and even their kids and make decisions about where to mentally place these people on our trust or respect scale. We can't ignore our nose in this decision making. Smell is an additional factor in "sorting" people as smell evokes memories.[1] It is neither fair nor accurate, but it is human nature and must be considered.

My husband and I live in North Myrtle Beach, South Carolina. One night, we decided to go to an impersonator show. This show released around 10 p.m., and there were few choices of restaurants available. We decided to grab a late dinner at the Hard Rock Café. When we were seated, our server, a young woman, approached. She was a beautiful girl, but she was covered from the neck to her chest and from her shoulders to her wrists in tattoos. In addition, she had piercings in her nose, eyebrow, and a multitude in her ears. I admit that our first thought was "We are never going to eat," but it turns out she was one of the best servers I have ever had.

Growing up in the restaurant business, I am a tough critic. She did an excellent job, and we enjoyed her personality tremendously. Still, I had to talk to myself about my immediate reaction and understand that as a person who grew up when tattoos were considered inappropriate, styles have changed, and I need to recognize my bias. Now, if this young woman had dirty hair, half-chipped-off nail polish, and a uniform that looked as if she had slept in it, no amount of self-talk would have overcome the impression that my food was being served by someone who was less than "food service clean." In fact, I may have left the restaurant.

EXERCISE: Think back about the people you see at work, on the street, in shops you frequent, or even celebrities. Consider what instant judgments you make about these strangers. Are they based on fact or a stereotype? Now think about what those same people are thinking about YOU!

Like it or not, our patients and clients are judging us, and that first impression is incredibly important. My wonderful waitress had to "dig herself out" of my mental hole. We have about ten seconds to hit the mark, and if we miss, it can take years to overcome the initial disappointment *if we are even given the opportunity*. It is here that company dress codes come to play.

Dress codes set clear expectations on what attire, jewelry, hair styles, shoes, and overall appearance are acceptable for work. Dress codes are not universal because your brand is not universal. The attire of the team should complement the brand you envision. The majority of our clientele were business executives, doctors, attorneys, and other affluent members of the community which made my first hospital like the "animal country club," so for the North Carolina summers, our team had embroidered tee shirts and for the winter, sweatshirts emblazoned with our logo. The customer service representatives (CSRs) wore business casual and were instructed to dress like bank tellers with white embroidered lab jackets over their clothes. The doctors wore light blue front zip smocks and business casual clothes with the men in ties. While other practices have a much more relaxed dress code with scrubs as the norm, the formality of our dress worked well for our clientele. Many studies have been done on dress codes in medical offices with some that tout white coats for doctors and newer ones stating that scrubs are more trusted. My thoughts are decide *your* brand, and let it dictate your dress code. One tip I would suggest: Incorporate your brand and logo colors into your dress code. The point? Starbucks' green is so imprinted on our psyche that we would know it if it was a big green dot instead of the full image of the iconic mermaid.

Digging a little deeper, what does it look like to drive up and walk inside your practice? Often team members park in the employee lot, enter through an employee door, clock in, and begin to work. Because we live and work in our office every day, we no longer notice the wear and tear on our furnishings and even our parking lot. It is always a good idea to drive up to the practice as a client would and to get an idea of your client's view. The same goes for the lobby and waiting areas.

I once visited a veterinary practice with one of my friends who was a sales representative. We drove into the parking lot, dodging enormous potholes. What was left of the parking space striping was faded. The shrubbery had overgrown to the point that it had narrowed the opening for the front door sidewalk down to a width of approximately three feet. To get inside, we had to squeeze past two gigantic unkempt bushes. Upon entering the lobby, we were hit with an odor that was a mix of cat urine and pine cleaner. Every chair had a rip in the upholstery. The walk-off mats at the entry were covered in fur.

Upon approaching the front desk, we were greeted by a CSR whose hair and scrub top were equally dirty. The staining on the scrub top looked suspiciously like poop. There were mounds of paper charts piled behind the desk. The framed pictures on the wall were yellowed with age and covered in fly specks. The posters taped to the wall were long out-of-date with curled and torn corners. The baseboard radiator was rusted from years of a multitude of dogs lifting their legs upon it. When we announced ourselves, the CSR stared at us as if we were aliens and turned away to ask someone else what to do with us.

As we waited in the lobby, I overheard some pet owners discussing how bad their dog's breath was and that they hoped the doctor would offer some solutions. They were eventually called back, and since the doctor never closed the exam room door, I observed the visit and saw to my disappointment that the dogs were not examined but were merely given a couple of vaccinations, and their teeth were never addressed. It was hard to hold my tongue and not say, "There is an excellent practice 3 miles down the road and they will help your dogs." My first impression in this case ran true—this practice was not only shoddy in appearance but equally shoddy in medical care.

Attention to detail shows in all we do. Consider a trip to Disney's Magic Kingdom. Every detail is considered, including the doorknobs and the manhole covers imprinted with images of Mickey Mouse. One of Disney's core values is "show." Walt Disney knew that when guests entered the theme parks, the first impression would be imprinted on their minds. Visitors will find no chipped paint, immaculate bathrooms that are checked every thirty minutes, no overflowing trash bins, not a single piece of trash on the streets, and you will never see a character from one themed area walking in another because Disney has designed a system of underground tunnels for employees to use after they are costumed. They never break character. Even the trees and flowers are chosen based on their appropriateness to the area and the theme.

Periodically drive into your client parking lot, enter into your lobby, and sit down for fifteen minutes, then look around. Find the dirt, the rips, the marks on the walls, the old magazines, and make corrections so the first impression you give is a great one.

EXERCISE: Drive up to your practice and look at the parking lot, shrubs, trash cans, and signage as if you are a stranger coming for the first time. Enter your waiting area and look at the walls, floors, doors and frames, windows, and furnishings. Consider the noises you hear. What do you smell? How is the team dressed? Make a list of what impresses you and what fails to impress.

First impressions are not limited to our first visual impression, but it is also our first verbal or even digital impression.

In today's tech savvy world, practices are utilizing many digital tools to communicate with clients. These tools are extremely helpful and leverage our capacity to serve people by taking over routine and redundant tasks. That being said, the first impression given by these communication tools should be that they are easy to use, enable us to quickly understand how to respond, and provide an immediate result to the task we are trying to accomplish.

This is certainly not a book about digital marketing, but having a website that is customer-friendly; ADA compliant, inclusive of all ages, races, and genders; logical to navigate; and displaying the exact information that the client seeks is an important first impression. If half of your doctors have retired and their pictures are still on the site and the photographs of your building are from 1995, it is more than time to update. As a new client, I want to be able to fill out and submit paperwork online. I also do not expect to have to repeat this process in-person. I want to be able to receive text confirmations of my appointment. I expect to be able to conveniently see my patient records via a secure portal accessible via my personal device. I want to text my provider a question, and I want to request a medication refill or an exam without having to call. If these services are not provided, my impression is of a practice that is way behind the times in customer service and possibly in current trends in medical care. At the same time, it is important that we remember our elderly who may not be comfortable with technology and continue to provide the face-to-face and pen and paper encounters they prefer. It is never appropriate to abandon a segment of your clientele because you find it inconvenient or more expensive. In hospitality, all are served in the way **they** desire and are comfortable.

6

You Had Me at "Hello"

Phones are still a vital part of our communication toolbox; not everything is done online. Training proper phone etiquette is essential to giving a great first impression.

In my early days as a CSR, I was trained to answer the phone by the third ring. The rule has now changed to answer on the first and have a plan by the third for someone else to answer if you can't.

We live in a world where the average person has the attention span of a goldfish. We are used to instant gratification when we Google a topic or message a company. Our expectations are even higher when we make the effort to call. Receiving a multitude of rings or a phone tree that offers no helpful or understandable choices immediately sets a negative tone. My suggestion is if you have a voicemail system, that you periodically use it to get through to your own office. Even better, have a friend or family member who does not work there run this exercise and report back to you on their experience.

EXERCISE: Find out how many hoops your clients are jumping through to make an appointment or to ask a simple question. Be a harsh critic, then fix what you don't like. I have yet to find a customer who said, "I love getting trapped in voicemail!"

My rule has always been to serve the person in front of you and have a backup for the phone. To me, the person who made the effort to drive to my office has status over the one who is calling. That is not to say the caller is less important—just don't break service with a person who is physically in your building to get the phone. And NEVER take a personal call from your cell phone when serving a client! This is incredibly disrespectful. You are showing that person they are not important or valued by you or your company.

If you have no other person who can answer the phone, it is appropriate to say to the person you are working with, "I apologize. I am the only person here today. Would you mind if I pick up the phone?" When met with this request, people are usually understanding and will graciously say they do not mind. Then answer the phone and ask the caller's permission to place them on a brief hold after first confirming it is not a medical emergency. (Over the years, I have discovered that the practice's definition of a true emergency and the client's definition can vary greatly.)

Speak slowly and distinctly when you identify yourself and your business and when you request permission to place the caller on hold. People are calling with a plan on what to say, and when you respond in a manner different from their expectations, they often don't listen, or they don't fully hear what you said. You may need to repeat your request to place them on hold.

Smile. It seems silly to smile when the caller can't see your face, but the caller can *hear* your smile; a smile changes the tone of your voice. Our first impression to our caller should always be that we are happy to have the opportunity to serve. People can pick up on your emotion by listening to the

TIP: Place a mirror near the telephone and check your smile and facial expression when you speak with your clients.

tone of your voice. Impatience, aggravation, and frustration all transmit over the phone as does kindness, empathy, and pleasure in serving. Make sure your tone matches the message you want to convey. When we answer, "Thank you for calling ABC Practice. "This is Debbie!"—they shouldn't hear in your voice the sound of "What a bother you are. I don't have the time or the patience to serve you." One simple tip I have shared is before you pick up the telephone, take in a deep breath. If you begin to run out of air in your lungs, you tend to speed up your greeting, and running through your greeting at a rapid pace gives the impression you are too busy to help your caller. Breathing also helps you center yourself mentally before collaborating with the caller.

Always identify your company and yourself by name. This is how we begin to build a relationship. I once called a practice who answered the phone with "Animal hospital." *How special and unique was that practice portrayed?*

We all love to have that special person on the inside of the businesses we frequent—the one we know will recognize us, know about us, and help us. It gives us a sense of security that we have a personal guide and someone to call on if we need assistance. Your goal is to become "that" person for many of your clients.

One of the most unique marketing tools I have seen employed in a practice involved the use of a large postcard with a group photograph of the team. When any member of the hospital worked with a new client over the phone, they circled their picture on the card, wrote their name under it, and mailed it to the new client with a statement that read, "Mrs. Jones, it was a pleasure helping you today. Remember my name is Toni, and if you need anything in the future please call and ask for me." Now, Toni was no longer a faceless voice on a telephone call; she was an inside connection that the client could call and even recognize when they walked in the door. Brilliant! In today's world, we can text a photo and a digital greeting instead.

When speaking with clients on the phone, you should not engage in multitasking. In fact, the ability to multitask is a myth. We are biologically incapable of multitasking. Instead, what we do is called "task switching," which is typically very inefficient. The brain cannot do two complex things simultaneously and do them well. However, we can perform an established habit (like brushing our teeth) and simultaneously think a complex thought.[1] If you have ever driven to work while trying to solve a problem in your mind and arrived with no memory of how you got there, you have experienced complex thought paired with a well-established habit. Attempting to multitask when serving others only leads to distracted work and unhappy clients who feel they are playing second fiddle to the other tasks you are attempting to perform. Focus on the person. Leave the other tasks until you are finished.

One challenge you will experience when attempting to put the concepts of hospitality in place will be overcoming your current habits. It is uncomfortable and takes mental effort to overcome your old patterns and create new ones. If you have ever changed jobs and found yourself mistakenly driving to your old job while lost in thought, you understand. Habits are neuropathways our brain creates to conserve energy. Unfortunately, the bad habit paths are permanently embedded in our brain, so we have to be wary of them popping up when we let down our guard. This is why smokers struggle to quit. Even though they desperately want to stop, they are pulled into old habits when they engage in activities where they habitually smoked, like drinking in a bar, after a meal, or on work breaks with other smokers. Their subconscious neuropathway is reactivated, and they pick up a cigarette. Support from others is helpful when you are working on building a new improved habit. I call this the Weight Watchers theory of habit change. We allow others to help hold us accountable until our new path is so ingrained that we no longer backslide. Great cultures do this for each other using kindness, humor, and forgiveness when we fail. Change is hard, but the results are worth it!

True confession time. I was terrible at remembering names. The famous Dale Carnegie quote "Remember that a person's name is to that person the sweetest and most important sound in any language" was trained in me at an early age, but there are many distractions at the front desk and names often got lost in the midst of finding a solution for a pet's or person's problem. Life got easier when client records could be searched by phone number, but that really isn't helpful when you meet them in the grocery store. Somehow, I could usually remember the pet, and it saved me embarrassment on many occasions. In his book, *How to Win Friends and Influence People,* Dale Carnegie writes a tip for how to remember names; it's called LIRA, which is the acronym for Listen, Impression, Repetition, and Association.

> **The first step in any conversation is to intently focus on the person with whom you are speaking.**

We often only half listen while we are distracted with the next task or planning our response. Instead listen as if you were playing the children's game Simon Says. The laser focus required to follow the Simon Says "Pat your head" type command is the gift we should give anyone with whom we are speaking. If your mind starts to wander, be aware of this, and mentally pull it back into the conversation. Other than being respectful, active listening is important[2] when seeking cues to diagnose an illness. It also stops us from making mistakes of omission. Distracted listening can cause us to miss important information pertaining to symptoms, medications, and even services requested. Practice active listening, and it will pay off in many ways.

Next, take a mental photograph or form a mental impression of the person. Keep in mind the location where you met them and the situation. Link them together in your mind. In veterinary medicine, we often link owners with their pets. I personally have been caught many times in a restaurant greeting a client whose name I do not remember but whose pet I absolutely did. Did they come in with someone you know? If you draw a blank, you can quietly ask that person to refresh the name of their acquaintance for you.

Find a way to repeat a person's name. I recently met one of my new neighbors while out walking my dog. We chatted for a few minutes, and as I walked away, I looked back and said, "Tonia, right?" And she said, "Yes, and you are Debbie, right?" This repetition and confirmation made sure we will both remember each other's names in the future. By the way, her dog's name is Fez, which I instantly remembered. If you are on a call with a client, it is a good idea to use their name at least three times in the conversation and especially when ending the call. If you didn't catch the name the first time, just apologize and say, "I am sorry. I missed hearing your name. Do you mind repeating it for me?" At this point, you should also reintroduce yourself so the caller can remember who they spoke with. When speaking with new clients, I used to end our call with, "Mrs. Smith it was my pleasure speaking with you. Remember my name is Debbie, and if you have any other questions or need something else, just call and ask for me."

Often, we are embarrassed to ask a person's name again, but forgetting someone's name in a conversation is universal and human. If we take the time to ask again the name of person we just met, they know we feel they are important, that we value them, and want to honor that by knowing their name. If a name is challenging to pronounce, it is also okay to ask if you are pronouncing it correctly. I would say, "It is important to me to get this right. Will you help me pronounce your name correctly?" It is also okay to practice it with the person. If someone has an unusual name, they know people struggle. Rather than butcher it, move into the discomfort, confess your difficulty, and get it perfect. People appreciate a genuine effort. In this moment, we also share our vulnerability, which makes us more likeable.

I met another neighbor who has an unusual name. I asked if it was a family name, and she told me she was actually named after a TV producer for *The Bob Newhart Show*. Her parents were watching it one night shortly before she was born and liked the name. Knowing the story behind her name makes it "sticky." We also connected by laughingly recalling the brothers Larry, Daryl, and Daryl from the show. I now easily recall her name when I see her. She had just adopted a new puppy named Harbor, and her older dog's name is Rocket. I recalled the dog's names because we live on the water, so "Harbor" made sense in that context; and Rocket made me visualize a dog with the zoomies running like a rocket. *(See what I mean about remembering pets' names.)*

> **EXERCISE:** Use the acronym LIRA (listen, impression, repetition, and association) or another tool to go through your day and make a conscious effort to remember people's names that you meet. Then at the end of the day try to recall all the names and faces. How successful were you?

One tip I have shared over the years has been when working, keep a pen and small pad handy, and the minute someone shares their name, write it down. (If you want to sneak and try this at a party, feel free.) I understand that the client's name is usually up on a computer screen, but writing it down is a memory prompt. It sticks better when more of our senses, like touch and sight, are involved in creating the memory. As I went through conversations with clients, I would often flip screens from appointment check-in to medical chart notes to boarding reservations. Keeping that name in front of me made sure no matter what I was looking at, and even if I needed to walk away, the name was available at a glance. It also reminded me to use that name in the conversation and especially when I was ending the call. When you use someone's name, it personalizes the call for them and for you. They become an appreciated human rather than a chore to be checked off a task list.

In veterinary medicine, sometimes our calls are urgent. Managing a caller whose pet has been hit by a car can be challenging. The pet owner is distraught, the pet is critical, and the CSR or technician has to guide this conversation while maintaining a calm yet empathic tone. Acknowledge the distress of the owner by saying, "I know this is frightening, and I am going to help you." Then move forward with instructions for transport, first aid, and directions to the practice if needed. Practice empathy first! Always get a call back number. On occasion, clients will call, an emergency situation is determined, and the medical staff is alerted, but the client and patient never show up. If you give them a reasonable amount of time to arrive and they are not at the hospital, call to see if they are lost, if the pet expired, or if they need instructions on handling the pet because it is uncooperative.

If you are not sure what the protocol is for various types of emergency situations, find out. To this day, I still remember the first "hit by car" case I participated in admitting. I had no training on what to do or who to call to help. I am sure that client received no comfort in having me attempt to check her in at the front desk. Fortunately for the dog, it was just a slight bump, and he was fine; but as a new employee, I was still left hanging out to dry because of a lack of a formal training plan.

Once the caller is on the way, you may need to take a short personal break. These calls are not routine unless you work in an emergency room (ER) so taking time to calm your mind and release the tension is a good idea. A simple box breathing exercise will help you relax. (See insert on page 44.) Then you can move back into serving other clients with a smile once your adrenaline has shifted back to a normal level. This also works with the client who is belligerent. Take that time to return to a calm state.

EXERCISE: Consider any urgent or emergent case you have seen. What could you do to improve the protocol to help give the client a better service experience? What training do you need to do so?

BOX BREATHING

Box breathing is known to help us bring our energy down to a normal level after a stressful event. The technique is simple:

- Breath in deeply to the count of four.
- Hold it for a four count.
- Release it to the count of four.
- Hold it for another four count.
- Repeat at least three times.

It is easy to remember if you envision the steps like the sides of a box with each set of four-count breathing as a side.

In busy practices, it is inevitable that we must place callers on hold. If you must, ask permission first. Don't be surprised if the caller continues speaking. Over the years, I have discovered that people who call a business plan their conversation ahead of time. When the team member answers the phone and the conversation doesn't go as expected, the client is frequently caught off guard. When you veer off routine, often they are not actively listening and, instead, continue their conversation. At that time, you will probably have to repeat your request to be allowed to place them on hold. Usually, they apologize and comply. Sometimes they continue to press their need. If so, you must decide if you can manage the call in a brief time then quickly continue serving the client in front of you. If not, you may once again insist about the hold.

If you do place a caller on hold, that call is your responsibility until another team member engages that client. The perception of hold time by the caller is vastly different than the perception of time by the busy person who answered the phone. Two minutes can seem like an eternity, especially if there is no music or messaging on hold. If someone has been on hold more than two minutes without getting a response from the person they asked to speak with, get back on the call, and ask if they would like to continue to hold or if they would prefer a call back, a text or an email instead. This way, if the caller chooses to wait, you made the offer. If they choose a different route, make sure you follow-up. Remember, this is still *your* call and your responsibly to manage. Just as if you were the host of a party where you would escort a guest in your home from one room to another, you must be a good host to this caller. You are their escort from the call to the intended party, and you should never abandon them to chance.

Perhaps the caller decides to leave a message instead. Do not assume the person they asked to speak with has all the person's information—no matter how familiar they appear to be. I can't tell you how many clients called my practice owner by first name, yet he had no idea who they were when they called. Clearly write the caller's full name; time of call; subject of call or question; best time to return the call, and in veterinary medicine, the pet's name they are concerned about. Always put your initials or an identifier to indicate who wrote the message, and have a designated area for messages to be placed. You can also take digital messages if you use internal message boards. Again, follow-up and make sure the person you took the message for has received it. If the person is not in the office the day the call comes in, give the caller an idea of when the call will be returned. Don't leave people in limbo!

When clients call us, they are looking for a solution to a problem. It can be as simple as they need a bag of pet food or as complex as a medical issue that needs to be addressed by the doctor. Our job is to guide that conversation in a way that is mutually agreeable.

> **Our job is to guide conversations with clients in a way that is mutually agreeable.**

Appointment scheduling is a place where untrained team members fail to be good "tour guides." Typically, in general practice veterinary hospitals, Mondays and Fridays are very busy. Animals become sick over the weekend, and pet owners are reluctant to visit the emergency hospital; so, they wait until Monday. Friday appointments are usually dominated by owners trying to get in before the weekend for problems they have been monitoring all week, or that is the day they get paid and have the available funds to make the visit since most pets in the US do not have pet insurance. Well-trained CSRs understand this and can steer clients away from those heavily scheduled days while also smoothing the schedule for the medical team.

Once it is determined if an appointment is needed, we can ask a preference of morning or afternoon by the client. Then we look at the schedule for the entire week and find our slow day and offer no more than two appointment slots on that day. If neither work, offer one more. Never ask the client what time they want to come. They cannot see our appointment schedule and playing a guessing game where they hope to hit an open slot is unreasonable. The reason we limit offers is to avoid decision gridlock.

When humans are tasked with deciding between too many options, they shut down and opt-out. Make the choices simple and few. Guide them to a spot on your schedule that makes your work go smoothly and helps you stay on time while it also accommodates the client's needs. It is always smart to sprinkle routine wellness visits in between sick patient appointments. Sick patient visits are unpredictable and are frequently the reason our doctors get behind. By giving them routine visits before and after sick visits, we allow them to have some "catch up time." Stacking sick patient after sick patient is a recipe for disaster. The number one complaint of all human and veterinary clients is waiting. Strategic scheduling may not solve wait times 100 percent, but it can certainly reduce the chances for doctors to get behind.

My advice to practices is to perform time and motion studies on their appointments and gather data on the true amount of time a certain kind of appointment takes. (See the Time and Motion Study template in Appendix A.) For example, a wellness visit typically takes approximately twenty minutes, a geriatric patient visit takes approximately forty, new client and new patient takes forty to sixty minutes if you add in a hospital tour, and a new puppy booster or a nail trim on a compliant pet takes only ten minutes. By using differentiated appointment times, we can avoid the stress of walking into an exam room and getting blasted by an angry client because they had to wait. Differentiated appointment times position us to better serve our clients and simultaneously keep our team happier. Today's practice management software can be set up with drop down lists that have preset time lengths for different types of visits. Take advantage of the tools you have to make your day more pleasant for all.

EXERCISE: Use the Time and Motion Study template from Appendix A to perform a study on your exam room flow for one week. Then average the times for each appointment type. This will give you a more accurate idea of the correct amount of time to allocate for each appointment.

Always keep in mind that our initial contact with a person leaves a lasting impression. The goal is always to make our client feel that we respect their time, that we understand and empathize with their needs, and that we are there in partnership to help them. When clients begin their experience with our practice on a positive note, they become more cooperative and are more enjoyable to work with. Working with clients who view us favorably certainly influences the enjoyment of our own work. It is human nature to want to be liked. Great hospitality can make that a strong possibility.

7

Active Listening: Observation, Anticipation, and Personalization

You may have noticed by now that I have not given you a lot of specific verbiage. That particular training is certainly important, and there is plenty out there to utilize. Rather than teach you what exact words to say, my goal is to teach you how to "think hospitality" and to use your people skills and imagination to create communication that connects.

In my mind, great customer service is like a three-legged stool. Without employing each of the legs, the stool becomes useless. The three legs are observation, anticipation, and personalization.

Observation

Human beings evolved in tribes. They are meant to work in collaboration and to be able to read each other's body language. In fact, we are so good at reading body language that newborn babies can differentiate and understand the nonverbal expressions of their mother's faces.[3] However, as instinctive as this is, the multitude of distractions in today's society often causes us to miss important cues into what others around us are thinking and feeling. This is why it is so important for us to minimize our distractions and to intently focus on the people around us. If you have ever felt uneasy when walking alone in the vicinity of a stranger, you understand how observation plays a role in personal safety. Devices like cell phones have certainly reduced the utilization of one of our greatest safety measures—reading the body language of other humans.

In a personal safety class I attended, the police officers stressed that in order to remain safe while traveling, always utilize situational awareness. In today's world, with the rise in mass shootings, it is even more important that we are paying attention to the people around us. Another important point was to always know where the exits are and to never hide in a place where you may end up trapped. Also, consider and take out-of-the-ordinary exits like a window if you are ever in a dangerous situation. For more information about how to best be safe, visit the Federal Emergency Management Agency (FEMA) website.[4]

Just like any other muscle we desire to build, the ability to read nonverbal cues can be exercised. The study of body language requires greater depth than is possible in this book. Many textbooks on the subject will be more complex than necessary when training client service. My favorite reference is *What Every Body is Saying: An Ex-FBI Agent's Guide to Speed-Reading People* by Joe Navarro. Navarro is an ex-profiler for the FBI and made his living deciphering the body language of criminals. His books are easy to read, and the photographs are extremely helpful. It is well worth your time to read and study his books.

For now, let's discuss helpful observations that will enable you to provide better service.

The first goal is to observe the person when you initially encounter them and gain a baseline for what is probably a neutral emotional position. At least, we hope they enter in either neutrality or in pleasant anticipation of a positive encounter with our team. It is immediately evident when an upset person approaches us. We read the tension in their face and in their body posture. This observation takes nanoseconds. Often, our reaction is defensiveness or flight. In these situations, it is important to control your own mental dialogue and understand that this person needs your help. Being empathetic and actively listening will help you succeed more easily than preparing for a fight. We will get into more detail about conflict resolution later, but for now, let's talk about the neutral or positive person.

People who are in a neutral emotional position usually have relaxed facial expressions and their lips are also full and lack tension. Shoulders are typically relaxed, and arms hang by the person's side. The eyes are soft, and the eyebrows and forehead are smooth. Everything in their body posture says they are comfortable. Ideally, you want your customer to remain in this posture or, even better, to begin to feel pleasure and start to smile. Happy people smile with not just their lips but also with their eyes. The eye corners will crinkle with smile lines and the ends of the lips turn up. You may even notice a slight bounce in their step.

> **A simple rule is when humans are happy, things move up, and when humans are unhappy, things move down.**

If you have ever been in the position to tell a client that their bill was significantly less expensive than they anticipated, you may have seen that little "jump for joy" in their step. The greatest example of these body posture differences is to watch sports teams leave the field. The winners are all jumping, smiling, and have their arms waving in the air while the losers bow their heads, drop their shoulders, and move slowly with great sadness to the locker room.

Nonverbal cues exhibit themselves at the direction of the limbic part of the human brain. The limbic brain is responsible for keeping us out of danger. It reacts in milliseconds when it feels we need to respond to a threat. The common limbic brain responses are fidget, freeze, flee, and fight.

When people feel uncomfortable, as they often do in a healthcare facility, they may begin to fidget. You will often see women fidget with their necklace, twirl a lock of hair, or hold an object like their purse in their lap in front of their chest. Men will rub their face, smooth a tie, or pull on the neck of their shirt as if it's too tight. All people will perform what is called a leg cleanse by rubbing their hands up and down their legs from hip to knee as if they were cold. When we observe these "tells" we can intervene and help soothe whatever is distressing them. Commonly, clients will not tell you they do not understand medical terminology because they do not want to appear ignorant. But their body will show you that they are uncomfortable or confused. By observing these movements, you know you need to restate your information in a more user-friendly manner along with asking the client if they would like additional questions answered. As a general rule, medical professionals should always avoid medical jargon unless they are speaking with another medical professional. I occasionally catch my own veterinarian talking over my head because he assumes I know a lot about medicine due to my many years in veterinary practice management. I am familiar with common matters, but complex issues are beyond my scope of knowledge so I will ask him to clarify them for me. Most clients won't do that. Keep the language and explanations simple.

Too often, we allow clients to leave our practice confused. It is then that they return home to ignore or improperly perform our instructions for their own or their pet's care. I will always remember the client whose poor dog received his antibiotic pill as a suppository!

Or the person departs feeling disrespected and gouged for money just because they were being asked to pay for services with benefits they really never understood. Compliance is always one of a medical provider's greatest challenges, and if we learn to observe humans for signs of confusion and if we clarify our message, chances are great that they will follow instructions as we desire.

Impatience is another common nonverbal cue that we can manage. When we observe clients who are checking their watch, rapidly wiggling or kicking their foot with their leg crossed, sighing heavily and pacing, we want to run for cover. Rather than avoiding them, we can approach them with empathy and information. As mentioned earlier, waiting past scheduled appointment times has historically been the greatest complaint of human patients and veterinary clients. Medicine is not always predictable, and urgent and emergent patients will occasionally be discovered during a planned routine visit. These situations often disrupt workflows and certainly appointment schedules.

When we observe clients becoming impatient, it is important to inform them of approximate wait times and make an offering such as allowing them to leave to run an errand or to reschedule. Some practices have even been known to give out gift cards to nearby coffee or donut shops to waiting clients. People appreciate when you respect their time. They also enjoy being cared about enough to have their emotions read, recognized, and acted upon *before* they have to say anything. Good observation skills will enable you to avoid having situations escalate into conflict simply by intervening when the person has shown minor aggravation but has not reached a highly distressed emotional level.

Another helpful observation skill is seeing deception. Medical personnel agree that people are not always truthful about their behaviors. I recall a visit to a large specialty hospital outside of Philadelphia. While I was there, a teenager and her mother presented their family dog for what appeared to be intoxication. The mother had just come back into town after leaving the teenager home alone for a couple of days. As the veterinary technician questioned the pair, she noticed the young girl's body language. When she directly asked if the dog could have ingested an intoxicating substance, the young girl fidgeted in her seat, refused to make eye contact, and turned her body slightly away. This experienced technician knew enough to continue to press the question, and soon the truth was revealed. The child had a party while the mother was away, and the dog had eaten some marijuana-laced brownies. The mom immediately okayed the necessary medical treatment, looked at her daughter, and said, "We will discuss this further when I get you home." The truth was revealed because of this astute technician's skills, and the dog recovered.

> **EXERCISE:** Think of a time you knew a person was upset before they even spoke. What cues did their body give? How did you react?

In 1972, psychologist Paul Ekman suggested that there are six basic human emotions: fear, disgust, anger, surprise, happiness, and sadness. Later, in 1999, he expanded his list to include a number of other basic emotions, including embarrassment, excitement, contempt, shame, pride, satisfaction, and amusement.[5] Every one of these emotions can be observed in the body language of humans, and as we learn to fine tune our observational skills, we can easily come to read those around us and react appropriately.

Observational skills can and should also be utilized within the team itself. It is a common occurrence for staff members to catch a doctor in the middle of a case to ask a question about a different client, to okay a prescription refill, or attend to some other minor need. This is often not a problem; however, we should observe our doctor for signs of deep concentration or hurriedness. In those situations, it is inappropriate to interrupt to ask your question. It breaks concentration and causes the doctor to have to mentally restore their thought processes pertaining to the case on which they are presently working. These distractions could certainly cause possible harm to a patient if they result in the doctor being delayed in providing care, inadvertently excluding an important finding in a chart note or mistyping a patient prescription. While getting your question answered may seem an efficiency, what you have in fact done is made your doctor inefficient by forcing them to restart the mental process of case management. Remember that humans are incapable of multitasking, so you are forcing your doctor to task switch. These interruptions can cause a task to take much longer just because of the need to regroup.[6] If you approach the doctor and they open their stance to welcome you into their circle, then asking your question is appropriate. If they are standing or sitting and you approach and they do not swivel their hips, shoulders, or head to look at you but continue to focus on their task, you should not interrupt but rather wait until their body signals they are open to your approach. It must be incredibly annoying to have your work interrupted multiple times a day, so no small wonder some medical professionals get a reputation for being snippy.

EXERCISE: Count how many interruptions you receive at work in a two-hour period of time. Have other members of your team do the same. Discuss this at a team meeting, and work to create a system to reduce interruptions.

As important as nonverbal cue reading can be when serving others, one of its most important aspects is observing mental distress. Human and animal medical care will always have dire outcomes that, no matter how much skill resides in our practice, cannot be overcome. Most people, although they may be upset, manage to move through the sadness and grief. However, working daily with terminal patients in emergency, oncology, or assisted living takes a toll. In veterinary medicine, we will occasionally have what we call "death week" where it seems all our favorite elderly patients come in for euthanasia. Unfortunately, this usually occurs near the holidays because it's the typical time of year when families gather, and as such, it is considered a perfect opportunity to have everyone visit their old furry friend before saying a final goodbye.

Our observation skills should be used to monitor those around us for changes in their baseline behavior. Appropriately intervening with compassion and concern when a fellow human is struggling can mean the difference in that person getting needed help. A wonderful resource for pet loss and grief is the University of Tennessee Veterinary Social Work website.[7] They offer multiple resources to help pet owners through the grief process along with a telephone hot line manned by veterinary social workers. Post the new 988 Suicide and Crisis Hotline number in your practice.[8]

Always keep several books on pet loss and grief available for distressed clients, and don't overlook books for children of varying ages. Many local funeral homes have licensed grief counselors available. Contact them and offer to share the names with clients. Many times, in the twenty-three years I managed veterinary practices, clients have called me for support because the non-pet owners in their circle did not understand the very real emotional toll losing a pet creates. They were met with comments like "It's just a cat. Why are you so upset?" Animal lovers know that losing a beloved pet can be devastating, especially when the death is unexpected. Veterinary teams have the opportunity to demonstrate true hospitality in these situations.

> **Understand your limitations. Mental health counseling is a specialized skill set. We can certainly be knowledgeable, empathic, and supportive, but we should share professional mental health resources with those people who seem to be showing signs of overwhelming distress rather than attempting to counsel them.**

The American Veterinary Medical Association has a free resource on suicide prevention and mental health for veterinary care providers.[9] For human healthcare workers, the American Medical Association offers an extensive website focused on identifying mental health issues in physicians and in patients.[10] Fortunately, veterinary social work education is becoming more available, and professional social workers are being hired in many veterinary hospitals to support clients and staff with the emotionally taxing events common in caring for animals.

Anticipation

I have always thought that this was one of the truly fun aspects of client service—figuring out what people might need, enjoy, and be delighted by. In the realm of medicine, a comfortable and inviting lobby with pleasant lighting, nice artwork, and attractive and comfortable furnishings with some groupings that allow for individual privacy and others for family groups is advised. The Cancer Center at Duke University Hospital has certainly done a beautiful job in this aspect. When you walk into the entry you are greeted with a lovely thirty-foot marble fireplace. The desk and wood of the stairwells are a pleasing midtone color that looks as if it belongs in a high-end spa. The floor contains a meditation pattern with inspiring messages from some of the volunteers who founded various support groups for cancer patients. When you visit radiology for mammograms, the spa theme continues with beadboard wooden walls, iridescent tiles the colors of light green foliage, seating that seems to wrap you in a hug, and carpet containing subtle leaf patterns continuing the theme of a forest meadow. There is a refreshment station for coffee, tea, and water. Even though all the women in this room are draped in hospital gowns, waiting for a cancer screening or to get their results, they seem to be calm and relaxed while waiting to be called back.

> **Not everyone has the funding to create this type of Zen space, but everyone can do something to anticipate the needs of our human and animal patients. Simple acts of thoughtfulness will fill the bill.**

For years, we kept inexpensive reading glasses in a jar at the front desk for our clients to use. A jar of candy was aways full to give "people treats" just like we gave treats to our animal patients. Before coffee bars in offices were the norm, our practice brewed pots of coffee and served it to our clients in the exam rooms. We knew that pet owners who were leaving for vacation were in a hurry to get on the road, so we called them two days prior to their reservations to review the requests for play times, special foods, medications, and any other instructions for their pet's stay. Airlines even anticipate delays and have small bags to give patrons with a toothbrush, comb, toothpaste, razor, and shaving cream for the unexpected overnight stay. A student told me a story of a trip to a Ritz Carlton Hotel with her mother. They took a long walk in the garden, and when they returned to the hotel patio, an employee was there with two bottles of chilled water for them. He said, "I thought you might be thirsty after your walk so I brought you water." Anticipation of need!

An important anticipation of need in medical care is having tools in place to help a client afford care. In human health, we have uninsured and under-insured patients, and in veterinary care, we have a majority of patients with no pet insurance. We should work with payment providers to help clients pay for the services we offer. There are many options. Some are banks with credit cards specific for medical care like the CareCredit® health and pet care credit card that allows clients to pay over time for all their pets' care. Others are auto drafting companies that auto-draft payments from checking or savings accounts similar to how we remain current with our gym memberships. Still, others will split the bill over several months on the client's existing credit card while the financial institution remits to the practice the total amount due. Anticipate that people may, at some point, need these services and set systems in place to inform clients of your payment options. I keep a list of charities and ideas for how people can raise funds to help them pay for their pet's medical care. This list has expanded and still lives on my website, and you are free to download it to help clients, family, or friends.[11]

Anticipation can be used when we design our offices. We can opt for wider parking spaces for people with pet carriers. It is difficult to get carriers out of the back seat without hitting the car in the next space if they are too narrow. Add an automatic door that's operated with the push of a button or a sensor for when owners have sick animals in their arms, and provide a covered area for rainy and snowy days that allows people with non-ambulatory pets to drive up to the front door and stay dry while transporting them in for care. A favorite small touch is to add a place to hang a leash when checking out at the front desk. Even better, check people out in the exam room so they are not being pulled by the dog or holding the cat while trying to pay. Plan on seating for all sizes of people in the lobby and in the exam room. According to a report from the Centers for Disease Control, on average, both men and women gained more than twenty-four pounds between the early 1960s and 2002. During the same time period, mean height increased approximately one inch.[12] If you are still using chairs that look like they belong in elementary school, it is time to invest in the comfort of your clients.

Let's face it—filling out forms is necessary, but we can anticipate and innovate. Instead of requiring an existing client fill in a form with their name, address, and other identifiers, give them a digital pre-populated form that they only need to edit or confirm the details therein. For this, you can use digital tools to have them fill out client questionnaires in a more efficient and private manner. There is no reason these forms can't be texted or emailed to clients to complete in the comfort of their homes and returned to the office before their visit. I would certainly prefer the CSR to spend time greeting and welcoming clients rather than handing them a clipboard or an iPad and sending them to the lobby.

And with these forms, anticipate that not every patient who visits your practice does so with the same knowledge of their familial background. To this end, ensure your patient intake form includes an option in the family history section for the patient to indicate they have no information pertaining to their family medical history due to being adopted. While conversations among parties associated with adoption are certainly more open now than they were in generations past, this is not the case for everyone, and not having this option on the form can be triggering for the adoptee who struggles with or who has no communication with their biological family. One friend, who's an adoptee and whose biological family doesn't even know she exists, shared with me there have been times when she's angrily marked a huge strike-through over the entire family medical history section of a form and scribbled the word "adopted" on it because she found, at best, the practice was inconsiderate to assume all patients are in touch with their family and, therefore, privy to such medical history. At worst, with no option to specify she is adopted, she felt overlooked or not even seen. To include on the form an option for the patient to indicate they are adopted demonstrates your practice understands that not everyone is the same and that this is a reality you respect and is one for which you have anticipated.

Other areas of anticipation are accommodations for disabled or diverse people. In Greensboro, North Carolina where I first managed practices, there is a well-known school for the deaf; as a result, many hearing-impaired people permanently relocated to our area. We had on staff a person who was fluent in American Sign Language who we would call upon to help. Sure, we could communicate with these clients in writing, but accommodating them with someone who easily spoke their language was so much friendlier. If you live in a community with a large contingent of people who speak a foreign language, then hire multilingual employees. Our bilingual team members often interpreted medical instructions for our non-English speaking clients. This saved their bilingual children from having to learn difficult news of a poor prognosis for their pet, then having to translate it for their parents.

EXERCISE: Go room by room throughout your practice, and brainstorm as a team what needs you anticipate clients may have and how you can accommodate them. For example: In the restroom, you might offer lotion, mouthwash, a magnifying mirror, and tissues. From what other conveniences or accommodations will your practice and clients benefit?

Let's take this a step further and anticipate our employees' needs. Anticipate a need for your new moms who need a private and sanitary place to pump. Plan refrigeration for your team so they can bring healthy foods and snacks. Some days are filled with unexpected challenges, so keep food that is filling, healthy, and portable in the break room for times when meal breaks are impossible. Have personal lockers for everyone. Ask your team what they would like to have. We did and our group chose a picnic table outside so they could get a break in the fresh air.

Personalization

How annoying is it to you to go to a place of business and be greeted by people who are using a script? It is obvious that a customer service trainer has been in, and all the employees are now required to use this specific script on every person who visits. To make sure this is happening, cameras are recording the staff's client interactions.

My husband used to go to the drive-through at our bank every day to make a deposit for his business. He was a well-known customer, yet every day, he was greeted with the same words and asked the same question mostly by the same teller. After a few days of responding that he did not have an interest in whatever loan they were selling, he simply quit answering and ignored the person waiting on him. Instead of greeting a well-known customer with something personal, he was treated as if he was a stranger driving up for the first time. Rather than promoting a positive interaction with the bank personnel, he, instead, left so aggravated that he came back to his office complaining. I am sure, when budgeting for and investing in customer service training, this is not the outcome the bank wanted to achieve.

In the exact opposite direction, my good friend's mother, Jackie, was a teller at a local bank for many years. She had a memory for people and a genuine concern for their well-being. She also had a great sense of humor and was a joy to be around. Even if there were three or four teller stations open, Jackie always had a line. The bank manager would often try to direct people to another line, but the customers would decline and patiently wait for their turn to be waited on by Jackie.

I have seen this repeated in restaurants, clothing shops, garden centers, and certainly in veterinary hospitals. Clients find "their person" and become regulars because these customers appreciate the individualized care and attention they receive. People NEVER like to be treated as if they are interchangeable. Humans are not cookie-cutter and should be served as the unique individuals they are.

According to an April 2020 survey by the world's largest strategy consulting firm by revenue, McKinsey & Company, "a positive customer experience is hugely meaningful to a retailer's success: it yields 20 percent higher customer-satisfaction rates, a 10 to 15 percent boost in sales-conversion rates, and an increase in employee engagement of 20 to 30 percent."[13] Doctors don't consider themselves retailers, but the fact is that humans judge us on how we make them feel no matter the business.

How can we make a visit to our practice personal? A simple first step is to remember and use their name as already discussed. But, digging deeper into personalization, we can remember specific things about the person we serve. If they have children, an inquiry about how they are enjoying college or their new elementary school is a good start. Maybe we expand on that topic and ask what their favorite subject is or who is their favorite teacher. Are they wearing a sports team logo on their clothing? We can ask how their team is doing this season. Are they reading a book? Ask about the title and author and if they like the book so far. Over the years, I have discussed jewelry, shoes, jackets, pet collars, books, nail polish, haircuts, new grandbabies, new jobs, retirement, new cars, classic cars, good restaurants, the price of groceries or gas, and the pain of moving or building a house. And with clients I knew well, I've discussed divorce, the loss of parents and children, cancer, heart attacks, and arthritis just to name a few. In fact, I even helped one of my long-time clients figure out why her husband had no appetite after finishing his cancer treatment. When she mentioned that Ted complained that food was unappealing because he couldn't taste it, I remembered my own issue with the same problem. I had thrush after receiving some heavy-duty antibiotics for a post-surgical infection. Everything I ate tasted like I had a mouthful of dry cornmeal. I suggested that Ted have his doctors check his throat, and it turns out I was correct. He started eating again after being treated. I couldn't have helped if I hadn't paid attention and known these clients beyond them being dog owners.

Keeping it personal doesn't mean asking invasive questions. It merely means that you actively listen to the clients, sincerely take note of what makes them unique, then you care enough to remark or act on those observations. People will tell you surprising things when they feel you care. Know the patient's history and age before entering the exam room. If they have family who are also clients or patients or have other pets, make an inquiry about them before you jump into "business." One of the joys of working in my first practice for nineteen years was watching children grow up to become clients and often seeing them become parents. How rewarding it was to have three generations of humans and multiple family pets returning to our practice over the years. Hospitality pays in retention!

One of the challenges all medical professionals face is getting people to actually administer prescribed medications and carry out at-home regimens. Paying attention to people can be an important aspect of getting them to comply with directives. For instance, when my mother's cat, Charlie, was diagnosed with diabetes, I was concerned that the severe arthritis in her hands would create a problem with administering his insulin. Fortunately, Charlie is a very chill kitty and will simply jump up on the table, get his shot and a treat, jump down, and move on with his day. My Mom and Charlie have a fine-tuned system. But, when he was found to have arthritis that caused him too much pain to be able to jump onto his perch, he was given a nutraceutical. He has always been a very picky eater, so he refused to eat his food that was now laced with the supplement—not a good thing for a diabetic cat. If the veterinarian had listened to my mother about Charlie's very particular eating habits, she would not have wasted her money on a product that the cat wouldn't eat, Charlie would not have almost crashed from missing meals, and all would have been better off. But back to my Mom's hands—her pharmacist filled her prescriptions yet never explained how to flip the cap of the childproof bottle so she could more easily open her medications. One day, I visited her, and while in her dressing room, I noticed all these open pill bottles. When I asked her why, she explained that she couldn't get them open with her hands, so she simply left the lids off. I flipped the caps to show her how to cap the bottles and easily screw them off. She couldn't believe no one ever told her. Me either. Paying attention to people matters.

One of my favorite stories comes from a famous New York City restaurant. The restaurant owner and chef, Will Guidara, walked the dining room one evening, greeting his guests. He stopped by a table of men and asked them if they were enjoying their meal. They all agreed that the food was exceptional and told him they were on a foodie weekend where they were dining at all the most famous restaurants in the city. They were leaving early the next morning and expressed regret that they had missed getting a real NYC hotdog from a street vendor. The owner thanked them for dining with him and immediately sent one of the staff to buy a couple of hot dogs from a nearby vendor. He took them into the kitchen, plated, and garnished them to his standards, then took the dish to the table. He explained to the gentlemen that he couldn't let them leave without this last NYC culinary experience. The customers were so surprised and delighted that even though they had just consumed one of the finest meals the city had to offer, all they could talk about was the hotdog.[14] That is personalized service! That is true hospitality.

> **EXERCISE:** Think of a time that a service person truly personalized your experience. How did that make you feel? Are you likely to return to that business? Are you likely to recommend that business to your friends and family?

Again, perform this same personalization for the team. Leaders should know their staff and spend time understanding their life goals and needs. Can you offer specialized training to a person who desires to learn a skill outside their normal duties? If it will help the practice, then there is no reason why not. At one point in time, I had multiple assistants taking online classes to become licensed veterinary technicians. Our doctors agreed to mentor and teach as did our already certified technicians. Not only did this increase job satisfaction for these folks, but we were growing our own experts—experts who were extremely difficult to find in our area.

Flexibility is another way we can personalize work for our staff. Rotating holidays, understanding family needs, and allowing the group to swap days off are all simple things that can make life better. I used to tell my team, "I can't pay you what other jobs pay, but I can make it fun and enjoyable to work here." Staff retention was record-breaking with many team members working in the practice for well over twenty years. Hospitality works for all.

8

Training for 7-Star Service

As important as giving great service is, setting up systems that enable it to happen is even more important. Credit goes to Dr. Cody Creelman for his 7-star service goals. When Cody opened his new practice, FenVet, he had a vision of what it would be like to come into his hospital. He wanted people to know immediately that they were in a special place with special people dedicated to caring for special humans and their pets. A few months before he opened, he asked me to facilitate communication and client service training to his team. Then, he proceeded to engage those team members in building the workflows and the systems that would allow them the time to fulfill the vision. The architect designed the spaces to be open and to offer the transparency Cody envisioned. Clients watch through glass walls as their pets receive treatment. There is no formal reception area as clients are greeted by technical team members upon entry to the building. The lobby area is even specially designed for training classes.

Cody knew that giving great service requires appropriate spaces and tools along with enough properly trained staff to have time to serve clients to the best of their ability. Technology plays a significant role in Cody's 7-star service model. His business is an unprecedented success with him showing a profit after only nine months in business. In addition, he built such an excellent reputation that he had eleven doctors waiting in line to come work for him. Now, he is opening an additional practice to accommodate the demand by both clients and potential team members to be served by or to work in an environment like FenVet.

Too many times new employees are thrown into the fire without proper training. Some sink, some swim, but all suffer. No one wants to work in a position where they are set up to fail. Improper training does just that.

The first step in training starts with a job description. We should never hire people without informing them of the tasks and behaviors we expect of them. Creating job descriptions where there are no clear tasks or expected behaviors already defined can be daunting, but over the years, my suggestion has always been to let the people who are doing the work build the job descriptions. Start a digital document, or if you prefer low-tech, put a notepad in the area where the work is performed and ask your staff to write down all the things they do in a day, a week, and a month. Then simply review the document and organize the tasks. Quite often, we find job duties being performed in the wrong department. This gives us an opportunity to make strategic adjustments and to put better systems in place.

Keep in mind that you can have wonderful, kind people and a fantastic culture but still have lousy systems in place that make it difficult for the team to perform at their best. The best way to create good systems is to allow the team to develop them. Outline the goals for service, then build the pathway that positions everyone on the team to know their role in accomplishing the goals.

A good place to begin is with technology. I once was the chief operating officer of a large mixed animal and emergency practice. When I began working there, my goal was to vastly improve the service that clients received. I discovered that the software program slowed down the ability of my CSRs to enter new clients into the system without a multitude of tedious steps. It was just as difficult to invoice and accept payment. You know you need new software when a client looks over the front desk and says "I can't believe how many keystrokes it takes you to do this task. That is ridiculous!" So, we changed to a new software provider and invested in training.

A piece of advice I typically give practices that are bringing in any type of new technology is to utilize the on-site trainer to train the team in enough basic knowledge to be able to work the system. Then, six months later, invest in bringing in an external trainer to fine-tune the team and the workflows.

When learning a new technology, people find a path that works best for them. The problem is that is not necessarily the fastest or easiest way to perform that task. Bringing a trainer back after the team is familiar with the new technology; has a list of tasks they would like to perform better; and is knowledgeable enough to understand the windows, tabs, task names, and other features is a wise investment in next-level competency. Making this investment actually increases the return on investment made in purchasing new technology. On its own, cutting a key stroke or two may seem insignificant, but when we multiply that by ten, twenty, thirty, or more people performing that task twenty or thirty times in a day, you realize a dramatic savings of time—time that can be better utilized caring for patients and caring for people. Today's practice management software has capabilities that most practices rarely utilize. Investing in training allows us to leverage this amazing tool to grow our business, educate our clients, and support our teams by helping them with templates, formularies, reminders, and integrations that make their work easier and that allow them to go home at the end of the day with all their charts complete. It can even set-up roadblocks to medical errors by not allowing someone to invoice a product to the incorrect weight or species.

As a minor but irritating example, I picked up my dog from the boarding kennel after his first stay. When I got home, I noticed I had been charged for a twenty-pound dog rather than a twelve-pound dog. Tucker's weight was in his record, and since I am very familiar with the software in use at the kennel, I know for certain that the invoice codes can be set up to reference patient weight and give an alert when an incorrect code is invoiced. This mistake caused me a phone call, and it took time away from the CSR with whom I spoke so she could make the correction at the kennel checkout desk and so she could make another call to me to inform me about the credit being issued to me. Correctly utilized software saves employee time and client aggravation.

Each department should have a list of duties ranked from beginner to intermediate to proficient (pro). Accompanying these duties should be a system of pay grades that parallel the skill levels. Often a challenge in small businesses is lack of advancement. People come in with entry-level skills and start at beginner wages but have no knowledge of how to advance themselves to earn more income. By developing a skill-based training list, a brand-new employee can see what skills they need to develop to reach the pro level. Keep in mind that these skillsets are not all physical duties like placing catheters or running the end-of-day reports. Behavior and communication skills can also be trained and advanced. A brand-new CSR certainly is not ready to take on the highly disgruntled client, but the lead CSR should unquestionably have those conflict resolution skills. **Never tie raises to performance reviews or employee anniversaries**. Instead, tie them to your practice's performance levels and personal growth milestones. I have encountered people who have worked in a practice for years, yet their skills do not go beyond an intermediate level because they didn't make any effort to be or do better. They were coasting for a paycheck.

> **Reward growth and increased responsibility, not merely longevity.**

When training new employees, it is important to not only have them work with an official trainer, but it is also essential that they are partnered with a mentor. There is a difference. A trainer is available to teach tasks, systems, and the proper use of equipment. A mentor is available as a go-to person when the new employee feels overwhelmed or struggles with their trainer or any other employee. The mentor can give valuable information about special clients, a doctor's preferred way of working, and even some background on fellow employees so the new person can avoid committing an avoidable faux pas.

Training requires planning. I have worked with practices that close for two hours every Monday to hold a staff meeting and offer team training. Other hospitals do this monthly, and yet others look upon training as a random free lunch provided by sales representatives. Schedule and engage in team training. It is as important to the success of your practice as scheduling patient blood work or surgery, and you can certainly make time for one if you make time for the other. It is a matter of priorities.

My last practice had eleven veterinarians and approximately forty staff. We were open twenty-four hours a day, and naturally, the large animal doctors were often out on farm calls. By January, staff and training meetings were scheduled and posted for the entire year. Departments met to discuss their specific issues. Each department received specialized training. The leads of each department attended all the department meetings so a cross-pollination of information and ideas occurred. It was our commitment to team communication and ongoing learning and professional development.

For new employees, start with an orientation to the building, a review of the employee manual (I give a test on it because people don't read it thoroughly), the rules about parking, tardiness, dress code, history of the practice, bios of the principles, who is their direct supervisor, who to go to if there is an issue with that supervisor, and then the most basic tasks associated with their job. Have a checklist. See Appendix B for an example.

People need to see they are accomplishing things, and managers need documentation of what has been taught and that the employee has demonstrated proficiency in their work. "Follow them" training is not a plan. Once the new employee has demonstrated an understanding of and comfort with a beginner task, the trainer can sign off that they are ready to move forward. We then move into our next list. These tasks build and expound upon the basic task list. Some new employees may quickly move through the basics and the intermediate lists and be ready for the pro task training in a short amount of time. Others may need to stay at the basic level longer before moving to the second tier. Trainers, mentors, and supervisors should determine if someone struggling with basic tasks should be kept and worked with more diligently or dismissed as a hiring error. A common mistake is to keep working with someone who will never be the right person for the job. It wastes the trainer's valuable time and is not fair to the employee who is a poor fit for your practice but may be perfect for a different opportunity. Even great hiring managers make mistakes.

When team members become proficient at all the training levels, remember to keep reinforcing your standards. If you don't use a skill frequently, it is often forgotten like algebra or a foreign language. You must keep practicing. Experienced new employees come in with their own way of performing their job duties. On occasion, these tasks may be inconsistent with your workflows and the employee needs to be retrained. Or, if it appears they have a better way to perform a task, consider integrating it into your training regimen. Systems need constant evaluation as medicine and technology change.

Hospitality, as mentioned before, is about making people feel important and safe. When several people on our team are inappropriately performing job tasks, it creates confusion, especially when new staff members are coming on-board and observe multiple ways of doing a certain task. This is not to say that the way someone performs the task is incorrect; it *is* to say that we should consistently train all of our team members to perform to your standards. This also goes for setting standard protocols for procedures performed by doctors.

As a personal example, I have visited a couple of physicians in a local general practice group, and I have experienced a range of different protocols for my routine physical exams. The fact that my nurses and doctors seem to be jumping around in no particular order leads me to believe that this practice is disorganized and chaotic. Unfortunately, this disorganization has greatly reduced my confidence that I can get adequate care in this practice, and I will certainly be seeking a new medical care provider. Not only am I looking, but in random conversations with my neighbors, they have also noted that they had the same experience and also left the practice. Lack of consistent team training is causing this practice to lose clients daily.

In veterinary medicine, routine care, like vaccinations, exams and spays or neuters, are items often shopped by phone. Without standards set by the medical team for the vaccination schedule, proper vaccines for location-based risk, and protocols involved in surgical services, the team is unable to accurately give price quotes to callers. Medicine is an art and a science. Doctors do not work exactly the same for complex-case care based on where and when they were trained. However, for these extremely routine services, a practice must have all the doctors and the team on the same page. The doctors must work with a medical director to establish protocols and fees and then train the team to adhere to these protocols. When clients ask a question of any staff member about these services, the answers must be consistent or confusion occurs, and trust is reduced. The more doctors on staff, the more confusion is created unless standards of care are set.

Once routine training at all three levels is accomplished, a manager should work with individuals to discover their areas of specific interest (pro- vided that it is of benefit to the practice) and invest time and resources into advanced training on these topics. A CSR may want to learn about social media management, or an assistant may desire to go to school to become a licensed professional. The manager could learn advanced bookkeeping, inventory management, or take leadership training. Constant training helps your team reach excellence. Sometimes you can even train them "out the door" when they are ready to advance beyond your practice. That is an acceptable risk. I have always believed it is better to have someone won- derful for a year than someone terrible or unengaged for ten.

9

Personality Styles:
Customizing Communication

Many years ago, I was fortunate enough to take a class called "Dealing With Difficult People."[15] Even though I had been serving the public since I was twelve years old, I felt that this training could be beneficial because my new boss was certainly challenging. He had a strong personality, with definite opinions about how things should be done, and he was also very tall, which made him even more intimidating. I felt that any tips I picked up in this class would be helpful. I was right. Learning about different communication styles based on personality profiling was one of the most helpful continuing education courses I have ever taken. I used this knowledge when managing staff and when serving clients.

Personality profiling is certainly nothing new. Documentation of the different profiles can be found as far back as 444 BC and credited to Hippocrates. William Marston, in his 1928 book, *Emotions of Normal People*, described four basic personality types: **D**ominance, **I**nducement, **S**ubmission, and **C**ompliance. These personalities styles have been expanded on in a multitude of ways, including Colors,[16] Myers-Briggs,[17] and even in Enneagrams.[18] As a fun aside, Dr. Marston also invented the lie detector and the comic book character Wonder Woman.

All these personality tests accomplish the same goal. They help us understand ourselves and those around us. People are usually a combination of the personality types. Typically, one personality style takes precedence over the others, with the secondary style being utilized in specific situations. As an example, someone with the Inducement personality as their primary and Dominance as their secondary will first attempt to charm the person they are interacting with into complying with their wishes. If charm has no effect, then they will attempt force by raising their voice and then using sarcasm or, finally, threats to get their way. The main thing to remember is that each of us is unique, but each of us has tendencies that are predictable if we know what to look for.

Let's start with the Dominance style.

If this personality style had a tag line, it would be "Get 'er Done!" In my mind, folks with the Dominance personality style are, or at least attempt to be, the ruler of their world. They have a strong need to be in control. As customers, they tend to want to dictate their service experience to suit their need for speed. Above all things these people hate wasted time, so getting them into an exam room and seen very close to the appointment time is a key to a smooth start. Think *efficiency*! Allow them to fill out paperwork ahead of time if possible, and don't spend lots of time on idle chitchat. Get to the point. Chances are good that any conversation will be more about them attempting to teach you how you should be doing things more efficiently rather than you instructing them on healthcare. You can recognize this personality style by their direct and often blunt speech patterns. They are decisive, so you won't have to be concerned that they waver over difficult decisions. They make up their mind quickly and move forward to the next task at hand. These people have a lot of self-confidence, often to their detriment because they want to jump ahead. Training staff members of this personality type can be challenging because they think they are ready for the next step before mastering the step you are teaching. Patience is not one of their strengths. Sometimes, if it won't cause harm, it is good to just let them learn by failure. Let them discover for themselves that they are not yet as skilled as they assumed they are. Then, they are easier to teach.

The Dominance style has a lot of good qualities. As clients, they are on time (ten minutes early is late). They are not overly emotional, so there are no histrionics when they get bad news. They are stoic until they are angry. Then, they are the most likely to push, yell, be sarcastic, and attempt to bully to get their way. They have an uncanny ability to see processes when it comes to organizing workflows. They like order, systems, and direct communication. You will often find these people in positions of leadership because they are not afraid to take a risk and direct others in their work. If we remember that under their pushy exteriors, they usually have good hearts and are willing to help others by using their skills to make tasks more efficient, we are better able to give grace when they get frustrated and begin to bark orders.

To help you begin to recognize these clients, I'll tell you about John. John was a longtime client of my first veterinary practice. He was a contractor with two beautiful golden retrievers. Every weekend John traveled to his beach house and boarded the dogs in our kennel. One day John called me to explain that he would no longer be bringing his dogs to our practice because it took too long to get them checked-in. Keep in mind that because we knew these dogs so well, we would fill out their boarding sheets in advance, have their records ready when John walked in, and, when we saw him drive in the driveway, we immediately called for a kennel attendant to be waiting at the door to take his dogs back. It was pretty efficient. However, because our boarding kennel was large and always full during holidays, John had gotten caught in the crowd and felt that we had become too big. I told John that I appreciated his candor and that, try as I might, I could no longer shrink our practice back to the two-doctor practice it used to be. But I said, "John, if you ever need anything in the future, all you have to do is call, and I am happy to help you." You see, John's only complaint was about speed. Ironically, only three months later, John, in his direct manner, once again called me to ask if he could return to the practice because the new hospital didn't know him or his dogs and he preferred to take the chance of being slowed down slightly rather than go to a practice that did not give him personalized service. I welcomed him home.

Our next personality style is Inducement.

If you have ever met someone who immediately engaged you in conversation, has never met a stranger, and is so charismatic that everyone wants to know them, you have been around a person with the Inducement style. This style has also been called "the influencer" and "the entertainer" because the person often enjoys being the center of attention. They are people oriented, while the Dominance style is task oriented. However, they love having people as an audience more than being supportive of others, as you will learn about with the Submissive style. You will recognize the Inducement personality style by their elaborate and often dramatic communication. There is a lot of laughter, hand-waving, and gestures used to punctuate their sentences. You may find this personality style in many of your sales representatives. It is certainly a positive attribute to be able to connect quickly with a stranger when you are visiting practices and attempting to bypass gatekeepers.

As clients, these folks are often some team favorites because they are typically fun, upbeat, and engaging. Frustration steps in when we attempt to educate or give detailed instructions about patient care because this style is certainly not detail oriented. In fact, details are often considered quite boring for these big-picture thinkers.

As team members, duties best suited to their style involve creative thinking. They flourish with posting on social media, taking photographs, and creating content that is interesting and appealing. These are the perfect people to work on the theme for your next open house or practice event. Whatever you do, don't give them a task that requires attention to meticulous detail, such as counting and managing inventory. They will be incredibly bored, and chances are good that they will become distracted mid-count and never finish—especially if they are doing it alone. In a veterinary practice, they make wonderful exam-room technicians. They have the ability to make connections quickly and a flare for explaining the need for services and getting agreement from clients.

When training this personality style, visuals and hands-on practice typically are more effective than reading. If they must read to learn, present content in short segments and test incrementally. They won't shirk from role-playing, and you will often find that giving them public praise is very motivating, much like the applause from an audience.

My client, Ruth, is the perfect example of the Inducement personality style. Ruth didn't just walk into the practice; Ruth made a grand entrance into the practice. You could hear her laughing in the parking lot, and we all recognized her deep, throaty laugh. She was boisterous upon entry, instantly greeting all our CSRs, then turning to any waiting client in the lobby to see who she knew. She always had a story or joke to tell as we checked-in her pet for its medical care. We rarely bothered putting her in the exam room to wait for the doctor because, within seconds, she would be back out at the front desk for a chat. Remember, the Inducement personality style hates to be alone. If the CSRs were busy, Ruth would visit with other clients, whether she knew them or not. Our doctors knew to first peak in her assigned room and, if she wasn't there, come up to the lobby to retrieve her. When it was time to check out, she left with as much enthusiasm as she had entered, and once she was gone, the hospital felt slightly diminished. I'm sure you have some "Ruth's" in your practice.

Submission is our third personality style, often called "steadiness" or a "relator."

When I think of this personality style, the word that comes to mind is "aww" because they are highly empathetic, relate to others' suffering, and "aww" is the first thing they say when they hear a sweet or sad story. Many people have this personality type in the medical field. Similar to Inducement types, Submission types are people oriented. They have a deep need to be liked by others and, because of that, will often fail to stand up for themselves, even when circumstances warrant that they should. They are agreeable and love to be helpful and supportive. In my training classes, I ask leaders to pay special attention to these kind hearts as they can be subjected to bullying by stronger personality styles.

As clients, people with this personality style are usually patient, understanding, and kind to those serving them. They pay compliments and, on occasion, bring cards or small gifts to people who regularly care for them. They ask a lot of questions beyond the medical reason that they are in the office because they love to build personal relationships with others. They have amazing memory for details about casual acquaintances that most people would instantly forget. Submission styles do tend to be very talkative. Busy team members have been known to avoid answering a call from these clients just because they know how long they will be tied up chatting. Submission styles are very patient and understanding when the medical team is delayed. When they do lose patience or feel hurt by an unfeeling comment, their communication is rarely confrontational, often passive-aggressive, and manifested in a negative social media review or an email to the boss after they leave the office.

If you have forgotten someone's name, this is the coworker to ask because they will certainly know. Submission types make exceptionally good CSRs because of their interest in people and building strong bonds with others. Their kindness is, on occasion, negative when people sense that they can be taken advantage of. *Never have a Submission type as your collection agent.* Their highly empathetic nature makes them fall easily for a sob story. They will take their training seriously, particularly when it focuses on the benefit to pets or other people. They will struggle when confronted with a difficult client because tears come easily, yet they are so nice that it is hard to be angry with them. Dominance and Submission personality styles often have tension. Submission types dislike blunt, direct, and unfeeling behavior, and Dominance types dislike emotional, touchy-feely expressions and long, drawn-out stories. It is best to separate these coworkers if each is strong in their personality style because they will get on each other's nerves.

My client with a Submission personality style was Candy. We loved seeing her come in the door because she was always so sweet and cheerful. We knew her well because she had a lot of pets and was a "frequent flyer." We also knew to give our doctor an extra ten minutes in the appointment slot because he was going to chat with her about many things other than just the animal she had in front of her. We made sure that we asked about Candy's family, her other pets at home, and even the horse that we did not treat. No matter how busy, we spent time chit-chatting about her day, and we never rushed her into an exam room because taking time to have conversations with the four or five CSRs at the desk was part of a positive customer experience for her. She felt so close to our team that we were some of the first people to learn of her cancer diagnosis, and we supported her journey until she unfortunately lost her battle.

Our final personality style is Compliance.

For this personality type, think details! This personality style is task focused and excellent at fact-finding and organizing. Label makers, folders, and lists are the tools likely found in this person's workspace. Skilled at data collection and itemization, Compliance-style employees are the perfect candidates for managing inventory, creating standard templates, bookkeeping, and organizing information and supplies. They communicate indirectly and include lots of details and facts. Questions are part of their approach to any action, and they contemplate the answers deeply before they react. They are slow to decide because they require a lot of time to gather information before feeling that they can make a well-informed choice. Getting things right is of paramount importance, and often they will struggle with decision gridlock and perfectionism. They will not be pushed into a speedy decision, no matter how hard you try. In fact, pushing slows them even more. Planners to their core, they hate surprises, especially changes to their schedule.

These are your clients who come with reams of Google printouts because they have investigated their problem online. They will clam up when confronted with information they don't like, and they can be very stubborn when you need them to make a necessary adjustment. To get them to change, you must use facts and present your case with logic and in a step-by-step format. Be patient; they really hate change.

Staff training for this type requires systems, lists, and reading materials—the more, the better. The need to be correct means that they will follow training protocols to the letter, and when asked to change to something new, they will struggle. Remember their love of details, so assign them tasks that require accuracy. Often, they will build a system that works better than a current protocol.

One of my Compliance clients was an older lady, Mrs. Mason. She was nice but reserved. I recall one Saturday morning when she brought her small dog in for a vaccination appointment. We had just launched our Total Quality Health Program, and I shared the information and benefits of additional diagnostics for her pet as I checked her in. Mrs. Mason refused the additional service but still seemed curious. Rather than give up, I placed her in an exam room and offered her a brochure detailing all the tests and the reasons for them. I suggested that she take a look at the brochure while she waited for the doctor to come. Sure enough, after she had time to read the details, which reinforced my earlier education, she was ready to say "yes" when the doctor arrived.

Keep in mind that these personality styles are generalizations and are meant to illuminate how people tend to react to the world they live in.

Humans are never all or nothing; they are a wonderful and unique blend of all styles and should be treated as individuals.

The personality styles are helpful as guides to serving others and in developing a better understanding of people on our team. Managers can use this knowledge to place employees in work tasks that they enjoy and in which they will flourish and grow. Service providers can use knowledge of personality styles to help clients get the experience they desire while providing information in the correct fashion for the person they are serving. Outcomes improve when communication and service experiences improve. Everyone wins!

EXERCISE: Have you determined what your main personality style is from the descriptions? Consider your family members or well-known clients. How would you categorize them? If you would like to take a DiSC personality profile at no cost, visit www.discpersonalitytesting.com, or find the link under the Resources tab on my website, www.debbieboonecvpm.com.

10

What Does "Great" Look Like?

As previously mentioned, it is rare in today's world that people receive a truly remarkable service experience. Companies like Disney, The Ritz-Carlton, and Nordstrom are famous for providing great experiences. Each has spent time defining what their ideal customer experience should be. In veterinary or human medical care, how do we define what a great experience looks like, and who is a great employee? The truth is the team builds and sustains the experience, so defining our experience goals and training our team to give that level of service are the keys to success.

I think the place to start is with the superstars on our team. We all have one or two people who seem able to manage the most difficult client, gain compliance from the most stubborn patient, and get rave reviews from the people they serve and their coworkers. Look at those people and define "great" for your workplace. You can even use former standout employees as your "North Star."

Here are the things I have always looked for in great team members:

First, great employees show up. They are 100-percent present mentally and physically, ready to do their very best to care for their patients, and ready to help others on their team. They bring ideas to the table about how to work better, smarter, or faster. They want to leave at the end of the day knowing that they did their best and left the practice and their world better than it was. The exceptional staff member doesn't rely on the leadership team to formulate all the improvement ideas, but instead they put thought into their work and seek ways to make it better. I always looked for smart people to hire who demonstrated the qualities of forward thinking and commitment to superior work. Great team members *care*.

Second, great team members are understanding of others. They give others grace and assume positive intent until proven otherwise. Sometimes hurtful remarks made on busy days mean nothing more than someone is hungry, frustrated, exhausted, or feeling overwhelmed. The great team member is mindful of this. They do not text their coworkers or manager at ten o'clock at night because it is convenient to them. They understand that in the few hours that coworkers are off work, they would prefer to enjoy their family rather than answering a question that could have easily waited until the next workday. A great team member understands that your client wants to care for their pet, their child, or themselves, but perhaps they are battling a personal or financial crisis you don't see. Empathy for others is the core of being a good human. Great team members are considerate and non-judgmental.

Third, great employees communicate. They respectfully speak up and act with curiosity in situations in which stress or conflict occurs. They acknowledge that all stories have three sides: yours, theirs, and the truth. Great employees seek the truth without telling themselves a story that makes others the bad guys and themselves the victim. You are only a victim if you allow it. Don't accuse—ask. Great team members communicate and don't ruminate.

Fourth, great employees are lifetime learners. They don't stand back and wait to be taught; rather, they actively seek to learn new skills. If education is not offered at work, they find resources on their own. Then, they live by the premise that knowledge not shared is wasted, and power comes from generously sharing what you know so others can learn. The great employee learns and shares.

Fifth, great people choose to live with a positive attitude. Neuroscience informs us that the brain seeks what we train it to find. If we look for negativity, we will find and dwell on it, but if we intentionally seek positivity in our day, we will train our brain to look for uplifting events. Great employees smile. Not only does a smile make others feel better, but it also releases endorphins in the brain that makes us happier. Smiling can set off a chain reaction of smiles, just like a yawn sets off other yawns. A compliment can do the same. Humans mirror the behaviors of those around them. Great team members seek to be happy and spread happiness with intention.

Finally, great employees have pride. They believe that their actions are the signature they put on their work, and they want to be proud of what they sign. Not every task is something they love, but they still do it to the best of their ability. In every business, there are fun tasks we love, tasks we are okay performing, and tasks we must do to keep the practice running. Personally, I disliked writing payroll. It was tedious and boring, but I wrote it early in the day so my team could take their checks to the bank at lunch. I was careful not to make mistakes because this was their livelihood. I accurately tracked the benefits because I wanted everyone to get the full measure of what was promised to them, and I did this every other week for nineteen years and never missed a payroll. I did it well because it mattered to my team, and I took pride in looking after them. Great employees care to do things well.

In a business, success rests on the performance of the people who work there. If you get the people right, success shows up. Only the employees have control of the culture. It is up to the leaders to find the right people, embrace and teach the core values of the business, and then allow the team to create the systems and culture to sustain greatness. Leaders must value people over profit. Profit certainly is important to keep a business running and paying its people, but it cannot be the only reason for a business to exist. The best leaders place employees first, customers next, and investors after that. Business is a long play, and it's a bad strategy to shortchange staff and customers or not invest in upkeep, team training, and quality equipment in order to show short-term gains.

Now, let's look at what a great experience involves.

Earlier in this chapter, I mentioned Disney and the experience it works hard to develop in its parks. One component that is stressed in the book *Be Our Guest* by the Disney Institute is the importance of process.[19] The writers equate process with the engine of a train. No matter how kind the conductor is or how beautiful the passenger cars are, if the train doesn't run, people won't pay to ride it. Processes include policies, tasks, and procedures that are involved in delivering service.

Having visited a multitude of veterinary hospitals and been a patient in several human healthcare practices, I can attest to the importance of having good processes in place to be able to deliver an experience worth recommending.

Wonderful experiences start with proper staff training as referenced in Chapter 8. Nothing is more frustrating to a client than to have someone who is clueless attempt to help them or, even worse, misdirect them. But beyond training is having a set of standards, core values, and a mission that the whole team understands and accepts. It is often surprising to people to learn that one of Disney's core values is safety, which is ranked first above courtesy, show, and efficiency. If a guest will be harmed by an action, the staff knows that keeping someone safe ranks above courtesy in that moment.

> **Every medical practice should build and rank their own core values list and then discuss with the team how they will be demonstrated in the business in daily interactions.**

Over the years, I have helped many practices build their core values. Sometimes this is challenging because it involves some deep emotional exploration with the leaders as to why the business exists. However, parsing out four to six core value words and then having the team discuss how they will live out the values and what actions they will put behind them helps get everyone paddling in the same direction. For an example of a core values statement, visit Appendix C for a list that I helped one of my clients develop for their practice. Their practice had been in existence for many years, so don't think it is too late to create this list for your practice.

As a consultant and professional writer, I helped develop the language for this document. The ideas and thoughts came entirely from the team. You can see that the values cover almost every aspect of the practice, from keeping a neat and clean workplace to never gouging clients with unnecessary services or products.

If you don't feel that your writing skills are up to this task, engage a professional content creator who can put into words the emotions evoked by your core value words and then utilize that language to reinforce the core values that your practice chooses to live by. Keep these and your mission statement at the front and center of each staff meeting and training session. They are meant to be used, not filed away in an employee handbook.

I think we could all agree that if a team demonstrated the core values from Appendix C, they would offer an exemplary client experience in their practice. However, this team also has a solid set of processes and standards of care that are written and taught to all new employees. Over the years, I have discovered that few hospitals take the time to formalize their workflows. Single-doctor practices have an advantage because there is only one way—and that is the owner's way. When the practice owner retires and a new doctor comes in, the staff is often pulled between how they have always worked and the preferences of the new owner. As hospitals grow and add more doctors and more staff, systems and workflows become more complex and often muddy. Taking the time to write out how the work is to be done is a good use of time, but it can also be intimidating to think of all the details.

A favorite tool I recommend is the exercise from Tom Wujec's TED Talk, "Got a Wicked Problem? First, Tell Me How You Make Toast."[21] This is an exercise in systems thinking. If you take the time to view the video, and I highly recommend that you do, you will see that a process as simple as making toast can be broken down into a very complex system. When I use this system in veterinary practices, I will typically take a common procedure, for example, a dog spay, and ask the team to start from the incoming appointment request and use Post-it Notes to create a step-by-step workflow for each department until the dog leaves the practice. You may think that this is as simple as the following: we answer the phone, we book the appointment, the technician checks in the dog on the day of the appointment, the doctor performs the surgery, the technician calls the client to confirm that their pet is fine, the client comes to pick up the dog and gets take-home instructions, and the client pays and goes home. But once you start developing this system, you find many branches to the tree as possibilities occur. For example, the appointment request is from a new client who was moving from another practice to yours. Now medical history has to be requested, and the client and the patient entered into the practice management software. Or, what if you discover that the dog is in season or its pre-surgical blood work is abnormal; you now have a new branch to the tree and more processes to be documented. This is an excellent exercise to utilize because it involves all the members of the team who take part in these workflows. It also reveals glitches.

In a recent visit to a new consultation, we were performing this exercise with the team. It was here that we discovered that two doctors insisted on a specific pre-surgical blood test and the other two doctors did not. This was a source of confusion for the technical team as they built estimates for their clients. Thanks to this exercise, we were able to confirm that the correct process was that all pets undergoing an anesthetic procedure would be required to have this pre-surgical test. Now the team is all on the same page, and they will all share with clients the same education about the surgical procedures performed in their practice.

> **Good systems create consistency of performance. Consistent performance helps build trusting client relationships.**

Clients like to know that when they visit a practice, the team is confident in exactly how care is to be administered. They want to have a reliable experience that creates a sense of safety and certainty in the competence of their care providers.

The final step in creating a great care experience is to engage the team in building what they would consider to be an ideal customer visit. Most of us have been on the other side of the exam table as a client or a patient. Reflecting on those experiences, work together as a group—even if it is seemingly impossible to do—to create a visit to your practice that would leave you walking away feeling like you discovered a diamond mine.

A common practice of all superior customer service providers is that they allow their team the autonomy to create a delightful moment. I was training a class in the Atlanta area several years ago when a doctor told me a wonderful story. His family had arranged to take him to dinner at The

Ritz-Carlton hotel for his birthday. They were finishing a fabulous meal when the waiter returned to see if he could serve them in any other fashion. Jokingly, the doctor said, "Yes, my kid has a rash on his arm. Got anything for that?" The waiter smiled and disappeared. About ten minutes later, he returned to the table and handed the doctor a tube of hydrocortisone cream. He said, "I went across the street to the pharmacy, and they said this was good for a rash."

This server was not only empowered to leave the dining room, go to a pharmacy, and spend money on a customer, but he was trained from day one to do so. The Ritz-Carlton earmarks a certain amount of money for every employee every year to use as they see fit to create these amazing service moments. They don't have to ask their supervisor. They are trained to think "over-the-top service" and are given the autonomy to provide it.

Over the years, my veterinary teams have hand-delivered medications to someone's house. They used our van to pick up skunked dogs and bring them to the practice for baths. My doctors made house calls to euthanize a special patient when we did not normally make house calls. They have entertained generations of children with everything from ice pops to showing them X-rays of puppies in the womb. They have celebrated the birth of children and grandchildren with "oohs" and "ahhs" over pictures and handwritten cards. They have shared the grief of the loss of a spouse by lending a well-timed tissue, a shared tear, and a shoulder to cry on.

Being great at customer service is not just what you say, it's what you do and how you connect.

> **EXERCISE:** As you go through your day at home or at work, think about how you could provide a little "magic" to the people you care for. It doesn't have to cost anything to bring joy. Try to create at least two moments a day that delight others. Note how this makes you feel.

11

Going Above and Beyond

There are a multitude of definitions of hospitality, but they all come down to how one provides service and cares for those they serve. I like this quote from Wikipedia: "Hospitality is the relationship between a guest and a host, wherein the host receives the guest with some amount of goodwill, including the reception and entertainment of guests, visitors, or strangers. Chevalier Louis de Jaucourt describes hospitality in the Encyclopédie as the virtue of a great soul that cares for the whole universe through the ties of humanity."

> **Hospitality is the virtue of a great soul that cares for the whole universe through the ties of humanity.**

Typically, we think of medical care providers as scientists and their teams as support for the science. But I discovered a long time ago that we are a service industry with medical care as our product. It behooves us to be good at both hospitality and sales. People are often shocked when I mention this, but we are working with people and their emotions. Both superior hospitality personnel and sales professionals have a deep understanding of how people tick and how to approach them in ways that build productive two-way relationships. Traveling and teaching enabled me to gather a multitude of good "above-and-beyond" ideas in addition to the ones my teams used. Hopefully, sharing them will inspire you to create your own. Remember that hospitality is a creative process, and once we begin thinking of inventive ways to delight others, the ideas just keep coming.

Above-and-Beyond Ideas

Welcome Letter. All new clients receive a welcome letter signed by the doctors. This letter comes as "snail mail" because it is a formal welcome and similar to a wedding invitation in that it deserves formality. It is written on the company letterhead. Tip: It is difficult to have multiple doctors sign these letters, so I used to have my doctors sign their name with a permanent marker in very large letters on a plain sheet of paper. Then, I scanned them into my computer and pulled them into my Microsoft Word document, shrinking them to normal-size signatures. This gave them a crisp, handwritten look. Just be sure that the signatures are password protected! We don't want those out in the world. See Appendix D for an example of a welcome letter.

Certificate of Bravery. I heard about this from a student and loved the idea, but more than that, the story she shared. She said they had a client who was a professional groomer. The client owned multiple dogs and was an excellent pet owner. Over the years, the client had brought all her pets to be altered at the veterinary hospital. Each pet had received its own certificate of bravery after its surgery. One day, a team member visited the grooming shop and on the wall, hung proudly, were seven certificates of bravery, one for each pet. Obviously, this small gesture meant a great deal to the client but also what a wonderful passive marketing tool for this hospital.

The certificate was a Word document with the pet's name, the type of procedure (surgery or dentistry), the doctor's signature, and the date. It was branded with the company logo, of course. It was given to the owner upon the pet's discharge. I remember as a kid going to the dentist and getting a certificate for an ice cream cone that I could redeem at the local drugstore down the street. It was a positive reinforcement for my dental experience.

Teddy Bears for Comfort. This idea was shared by my friend Emma, a Certified Veterinary Practice Manager. Emma was running a large ER and specialty practice, and she noticed that children would often cry when leaving their pet for treatment. She arranged to purchase a bunch of teddy bears that had been donated to the local Goodwill, and she used them to "make a trade." When the kids would cry as their pet was hospitalized, she would offer to trade the teddy bear for the length of the pet's stay, then trade it back when the pet returned home. This worked wonders for the tears, but she did note that often the teddy bears did not return. In another use, she would have the pet owners choose a teddy bear to comfort their sick pet (just so long as it was not there for ingesting teddy bears!). They were instructed to hold it while the team discussed the treatment plan and then they all walked back to the kennel area and "tucked in" the pet with the teddy. It smelled like the owners, and the pets seemed happier, as did the clients. Perception of caring was shown in this gesture of kindness.

People and Pet Treats. For years our hospital kept a candy jar at the front desk filled with chocolate, mints, gum, and other assorted wrapped candies. The jar was labeled "People Treats," and clients knew to help themselves. If the jar didn't have much candy left or it got down to the low-value candy, our clients would remark that we needed to make a trip to the store. This little bite of happiness was so well-known by our clients that, one day, a mom came to get her dog, and, before she left the car, her kids said, "Don't forget to get us some candy." We also kept cat and dog treats in envelopes for clients and our team to share with our patients. Everyone got a treat! Small surprises can make big impressions.

Keep Memories in Scrapbooks. In my twenty-three years as a manager, the number of cards, photos, and letters of gratitude and appreciation received by my practices were innumerable. This is not uncommon when clients perceive that they are truly cared about. I kept two different scrapbooks. The first contained the letters and notes of appreciation. On the hard days, anyone could look through this book and see the impact on families that our team had made over the years. It could be a real ego boost after a difficult client encounter or the death of a patient. The second scrapbook contained photos that our clients had sent over the years in cards. Because we were a long-established practice, it was possible to see children and pets grow up before your eyes in these pictures. There were photos of many of our favorite people and patients, some of whom were no longer with us but who still lived fondly in our memories. These scrapbooks were available for clients to view. Clients were always delighted that we cared enough to archive the pictures they had sent. Memories connect us. You can also use digital frames, but make sure to unplug them after closing because they tend to be a fire hazard.

Give Practice Tours. One hard-and-fast rule in my practice was to be prepared to give a tour of the entire facility at any and all times ... without warning. And we did. Cleanliness, order, and organization increase efficiency and are mentally less stressful than working in a cluttered mess. The mind appreciates having few things to view, sort, and ponder. It is amazing that a client can frequent a veterinary practice for years yet never have seen the working area. If you are ever a little behind in your appointment schedule, giving a hospital tour is a great way to occupy a waiting client and share how impressive your practice is from the technical side. As clients toured through the treatment area, grooming room, boarding kennels, X-ray room, and surgical suite, they were astounded at the complexity of the equipment used to provide care for their animal. One client exclaimed, "This is like a hospital on TV!" The perception of value is greatly increased when they understand that you work with more than a stethoscope, thermometer, needle, and syringe.

Follow-Up Check-Ins. When we discharge a patient and never call to see how they are doing at home, we lose a prime opportunity to show that we genuinely care. Practice management software can be set up to automate a list of calls, texts, or emails generated by particular service codes. It is typical in some practices to call the next morning after a procedure, but are we taking the next step by calling to find out how that ear medication is working three days into treatment? Or if a diet change is causing any gastrointestinal distress? Or if an eye ointment is even possible to administer? I will always remember how impressed my husband was with his endodontist when the doctor called him at nine o'clock the night after his root canal. It was a WOW moment.

Holiday and Birthday Cards to Clients and Pets. In veterinary medicine, getting a pet's birth date is a standard part of medical record keeping. I believe it is the same for human medicine. Every year our hospital sent out more than 500 holiday cards thanking our clients for their support in the past year. Since we can't know the religious beliefs of all our clients, a card of thanks and well wishes for a new year is better than a traditional Christmas or Hanukkah card. Your practice management software can generate a list by sales, date of first visit, or any other criteria you choose, or you can decide to send one to all your clients. Some businesses choose to send

Thanksgiving cards in November. Keep a list of all the clients who send you cards and make sure that they are on your list. Many of the reminder-provider companies offer birthday cards as an option. I enjoy getting cards from my bank, my dentist, and my vet.

Weather Prep. Being located in upper North Carolina, our practice experienced all types of weather. Rain, hail, snow, sleet, ice, hurricanes, tornadoes, thunderstorms—we got it all. On those cold snowy or rainy days, we kept big golf umbrellas in a stand and walked our client and their pets to the cars. Occasionally, if it was snowing a lot, we would bring warm towels from the clothes dryer up to the reception desk to offer to clients as they came in shaking off the snow. There is really nothing that feels more comforting than a warm towel when you are chilled to the bone. We kept nice towels for this—not the ones with bleach holes and stained with silver nitrate or ... well, you can guess the possibilities. When I was working on planning my last practice building project, I insisted on a porte cochère so clients could drive up and be covered when transporting injured animals from their vehicle. We also added an automatic door with a button (similar to a handicap button) that you could push with a hip if your arms were full.

Playing Doctor. As old-school X-ray machines are replaced by modern digital units, many practices have leftover X-ray viewer boxes. One of the most delightful uses that I have seen of these outdated pieces of equipment was hanging them at child height in examination rooms with a toy stethoscope, a child's doctor lab coat, and a pretend medical chart. An old X-ray is hung on the viewer, and the child is allowed to play doctor while the parents are educated about health issues. I have also seen these viewers used outside of exam rooms with welcome notes, written on the screen with an erasable marker, to the client and patient who will be entering.

First-Visit Keepsakes. Whether a child, a puppy, or a kitten, the first visit to the doctor is a memorable event. Arrange to take pictures of these new additions to your practice to share with the parents. In fact, how much fun is it to take pictures on recurring visits as these little ones grow? Share these photos privately with parents, ideally utilizing the client's cell phone to capture the moments for privacy's sake. In the animal world, these are wonderful photographs to share and celebrate on social media (with the owner's permission, of course). You can also do this for the first grooming—just like baby's first haircut—and save a few locks of hair for the scrapbook.

Farewell Keepsakes. Saying goodbye to our pet family member is always hard, but having a thoughtful keepsake acknowledges the human–animal bond. Many veterinary hospitals create clay paw prints for their clients. Kits are available in craft stores and also through veterinary distribution companies. But one of my favorite keepsakes is the nose print. Similar to a fingerprint, a pet's nose is unique. People spend much more time looking at their pet's face than they do their paws, so the nose print is much more familiar.

Simply take scrapbook paper, divide the sheet into quarters, and touch the inked nose to the paper. When done well, you will see the nose and the whiskers. Then, have someone with nice handwriting write the pet's name on the card with a calligraphy pen. The nose prints can be framed or placed in a scrapbook. In addition, we can clip a small lock of hair and place it into an empty, clear, and clean injectable drug or vaccine vial and reseal the top. Tie a ribbon around the top of the bottle and gift this, the nose print, a sympathy card from the team, and the pet's ashes, if they are returned through your practice. Place all this in a small, subdued-color gift bag. Another lovely touch is to place a packet of forget-me-not flower seeds in the bag to be planted in honor of the pet and a pack of small tissues for the tears that will certainly come when you present this package to the owner. If you have a relationship with a local grief counselor or veterinary social worker, you can add the contact information in the package or include an offer of links to books on grief. We kept these books in our library so clients could borrow them.

Sympathy cards are absolutely appropriate when a pet dies, but make sure the card goes out within one to two days. Waiting a week or more to get everyone to sign it only reopens old wounds when it is received. If you want to take it up a notch, arrange with a local florist to send a small floral arrangement to the pet owner's home. I think human doctors should certainly do this when one of their patients passes away.

Use Low-Stress Techniques. Functional MRIs have taught us the influence that fear has on our reactions. Medical visits are often painful, by no choice of the provider, but techniques have been developed to distract and redirect our brain from dwelling on the bad by reinforcing the good. My childhood dentist did this with the ice cream cone and being a wonderfully patient and kind person. Veterinarians do this with low-stress[22] and Fear

Free®[23] techniques. In researching how human doctors help their patients alleviate stress, it seems that the majority of the advice is to give drugs. Hopefully, with the lessons in hospitality discussed in this book, human medical care can learn from veterinarians trained in animal behavior about creating positive visits for people so they don't continue to create negative experiences that, over time, build into crippling phobias. After all, humans are just animals at the top of the food chain, and our limbic brain reactions are similar to our animal companions. Common human fears are fear of needles, fear of pain, fear of a poor diagnosis, fear of doctors, and fear of dental care. The Cleveland Clinic highlights some causes of the fear of doctors:[24]

> Children may develop a fear of doctors because they associate the doctor's office with getting shots for vaccinations. This fear may carry over into adulthood.
>
> You may be more likely to have a fear of doctors or medical tests if you:
>
> - Had multiple doctor visits and tests as a child to manage a health condition.
> - Received subpar medical care or had a bad experience with your doctor.
> - Have a chronic condition, like diabetes, or a life-threatening disease, like cancer, that requires frequent, sometimes painful, tests or treatments.
> - Received bad news from your doctor regarding your health or the health of a loved one.
> - Served as a caregiver, accompanying a loved one to frequent doctor visits and tests.
> - Lost a loved one to a medical condition or accident while the person was receiving care from a doctor.
> - Have a family history of phobias or anxiety disorder.

Many of my veterinary communication class attendees tell me stories of children bursting into tears at the veterinary office because they think they are at the pediatrician. We can certainly do better!

Community Events. Practices should always remember that they are based in communities. Creating and participating in community events is a great way to bond with your clients. Fundraisers, open houses, school outreach, inviting school groups and Boy and Girl Scout troops for clinic tours and show-and-tell days are all good ways to connect with the people in your area. One of my students shared the story of their practice outreach. There was a very popular local farmers market that occurred during the spring and summer. Knowing that people would bring their pets to the market and that it was usually very warm, the student set up a shaded booth with a cooling station. They had pools of water, fans, and buckets for the dogs to drink from, and they passed out branded information on heat stroke and how to avoid it.

My first practice held a fundraiser event for the Friends of Animals Foundation. We collaborated with local artists and crafters and hung their work in our practice to temporarily replace our art. The artists agreed to donate a percentage of their sales to the cause. One of our doctors was a talented musician, and we had him play at the event, along with a few other client volunteers. We set up tours of the practice, with team members stationed at various points on the tour to explain the equipment and the work performed in each area. It was a fun day for all.

My practice owner helped create a coalition of business owners to transform an abandoned railroad track that was behind our office. The coalition created a walking and biking trail that eventually connected to span the city.

Our team took a vote and decided to participate in the Heart Walk for the American Heart Association. I designed team T-shirts with the slogan "Walk your dog. It's good for your heart." We dedicated our walk to one of my staff's dads who had heart issues and to a client who had a heart transplant. Our small team of 20 raised more than $2,000, coming in second place behind the local hospital, which had 2,000 employees. (We also won the T-shirt competition.)

Small businesses can have big impacts. As a bonus, we also took with us two greyhounds from the Oak Ridge Greyhound Rescue to publicize the availability of these wonderful dogs for adoption. A photo of our team at this event still sits proudly on my bookcase.

My next practice managed the animal shelter for the county, and it was in desperate need of expansion and upgrades. The team started a fundraising drive by selling paper paw prints for one dollar to clients as they checked out. We placed them all around the front desk and lobby and raised quite a bit of money. One of my doctors was very involved with the shelter, and, with his help, the county finally built a brand-new shelter with four times the existing capacity as the original. When I started there, the shelter didn't even have a phone number to call. I was very proud of what we accomplished.

Food Drives. In a 2021 United States Department of Agriculture (USDA) study[25], it was found that 33.8 million people in the United States lived in food-insecure households. Food insecurity is described as limited or uncertain access to adequate and affordable nutritious foods, and it is a major public health concern because it leads to other medical issues. Pets also live in many of these households. Practices can help! During times of disaster, we commonly see bins collecting food items, but this is a chronic need in most communities. Set up donation bins, offer to collect donations, or go work at a food bank or homeless shelter as a group. These events help teams bond and share the care that we bring to our patients with our communities.

Adopt a Soldier (or Two). Supporting our armed forces is a great way to show appreciation for the people who risk their lives so that we can be protected from harm. Perhaps you have a client who is in the military. There is no reason you can't pick them. You can allow clients and staff to donate items, send postcards with good wishes, and share your "adopted" soldier with your entire practice and client base on social media. Gather requested items and ship them out. Veterinarians can adopt canine officers, firehouse dogs, and so on. Be creative!

Team Training. The most important bonding idea is to train your team to "think hospitality" and constantly reinforce those skills. Reward team members who get compliments from clients as often as those who perform great medical skills.

EXERCISE: Brainstorm some unique bonding ideas with your team. What would you appreciate as a customer?

12

No Judgment Zone

You will find biases and norms in any society and in any country in the world. Often, our biases are minor, like preferring certain hair styles or clothing and expecting those around us to comply with those norms. But at other times, our biases cause us to lump a category of people into a stereotype and then treat them differently because of our misconceptions. As you read in my story about my tattooed waitperson, I immediately lumped her into a stereotype of youthful inefficiency, which turned out to be grossly incorrect.

In a 2021 article in *Medical News Today*, the author explains that implicit biases can often get in the way of specific groups of people being served by medical care providers.[26] Implicit biases often run under our personal radar because, by its very definition, we are unaware of the existence of these biases in our subconscious. In fact, they can even be in direct opposition to our conscious beliefs. Therefore, we form negative associations with certain groups of people. There has been a heightened awareness of these biases, thanks to recent events bringing them to the forefront and highlighting a much-needed dialogue about conscious awareness of implicit bias.

As a child raised in the South, it would follow that I would have an implicit bias against Black people. However, because I spent a great deal of time—from babyhood to college age—in the kitchen of a restaurant manned by people of color, the results from my Harvard Implicit Association Test

(IAT)[27] test for race shows that I have little implicit bias. But even with my background, it does exist. I would certainly not say that I did not encounter people in my daily life who were not only biased but also incredible bigots (some of them even were relatives), but because of my parents' attitudes towards and appreciation for people of all colors, I learned instead to see those bigots as unenlightened and to never model my behavior or thoughts after theirs. Because I also know that I do have some small implicit bias, I can catch and correct my brain when it tries to jump into stereotyping. I highly recommend that you explore taking the Harvard IAT, as it is quite illuminating. There are tests for race, gender, religion, sexual orientation, age, presidents, disabilities, weapons, and weight. The results are sometimes surprising, and I challenge you to learn about your implicit biases, just as I learned about mine. The results are given immediately, and you are anonymous as the tester.

When, as a speaker, I began to travel the country, I discovered different implicit biases based on geographic location. In some states, there were biases against Asian Americans, while in others, there were biases against Latinos, Native Americans, and Native Hawaiians or Pacific Islanders. All this made me scratch my head because, to me, they all looked like ... people.

Growing up during the Civil Rights Movement and knowing both white members of the National Guard and Black civil rights marchers have helped me better understand the social movement around race. I was very young, but I have always been a "buck-the-system" kind of girl, so I listened intently to Dr. King but more so to the Black people with whom I had grown up. They told me what it was like to be Black and live having to always watch your back. Tom Haith was the manager of our restaurant after my father died. He had come to work for my dad at the age of fifteen and never left until my mom closed the restaurant and retired some forty years later. Tom always called me "sis" because we really were raised in the same kitchen. He used to say, "Sis, a Black man has to be twice as good to get to the same place as a white man." We had this conversation in the 1970s. It seems irrational to think that we are still having it today, but we are.

> **People who think that they have no biases and "don't see color" are deluding themselves.**

Our senses are automatically registering information about others like skin and hair color, weight, height, and attire. Self-awareness is what is required to overcome the biases we really don't want ourselves to have. Most people want to be kind, good, and fair. Their brain and background are tripping them up. We have all heard the expression "you don't know what you don't know." **Unless you start to pay attention and learn about how your brain works and how your upbringing or social groups influence your unconscious reactions, you will never be the person you envision yourself to be.** Once you know, you can't unknow, and that is when the light comes in and you can catch and stop your unruly brain from running down an inaccurate path of prejudice.

Prejudice is not just about race, but it can also be about gender, weight, education levels, socioeconomic levels, sexual identity, age, and ableism. When you begin to think with a hospitality mindset, you acknowledge that you could have biases and work with intentionality to make ALL people feel welcome. A 2022 *New England Journal of Medicine* article states that "in medicine, bias-driven discriminatory practices and policies not only negatively affect patient care and the medical training environment but also limit the diversity of the healthcare workforce, lead to inequitable distribution of research funding, and can hinder career advancement."[28]

I'll share with you a story about socioeconomic bias in veterinary medicine.

One Saturday morning, a man came into our veterinary hospital wearing worn overalls and an equally tattered hat. He was carrying an injured chicken under his arm, and he was seeking medical care for the bird. The team took a brief history and discovered that the chicken had attempted to cross the road and had been hit by a car. It appeared as if it had a broken leg. We put the man and the chicken into the examination room and proceeded to diagnose the problem. The fracture was confirmed, our surgeon was consulted, and it was determined that the chicken would need an orthopedic pin placement in order to repair its leg. Even though this was many years ago, the surgery was considered expensive at around $700. Despite the appearance of this client, who looked as if he did not have a nickel in his pocket, our team shared the treatment plan and the estimate of cost. To our surprise, the treatment plan was approved, and the chicken received its needed surgery. Upon the patient's discharge, we discovered that the client had taken this chicken to two other veterinary practices that had discouraged him from having the animal treated, one even suggesting that he kill it and have it for dinner! We then discovered that this man was a physician who worked out of our local hospital. He was so impressed with the work that we did that he transferred all of his pets to our practice and referred many of his hospital associates. If we had judged him by his appearance, we would have not only not helped Henrietta the chicken, but we also would have lost what became an excellent client and innumerable new clients from his referrals to us.

> **EXERCISE:** Can you recall a time when you judged a person as unwilling or unable to afford the care you offered, and they ended up surprising you? What bias did you have towards that person? How can you work to avoid that going forward?

Because one of the legs of the hospitality stool is anticipation, we should understand our clients' implicit biases and work to overcome them. Thanks go to my friend, Elle, for this next enlightening story.

As a Black woman, Elle shared that her community can have a general mistrust of doctors, hearkening back to the infamous syphilis study at Tuskegee or the collection and use of a Black woman's, Henrietta Lacks, cells by a hospital without obtaining Lacks' consent in the 1950s. Additionally, oftentimes people of color have their problems dismissed or inadequately treated because doctors have implicit biases that assume that these patients won't listen or follow through with recommendations or aftercare.[29] Furthermore, the significantly higher maternal mortality rates among Black women in contrast to other women weighed heavily on her mind. But when Elle went into labor at the birth of her first child, the medical team in no way acted with any respect for or acknowledgment of these underlying concerns nor did they address her obvious anxiety. It was already emotionally taxing for her because, for a number of reasons, the only family that could be with her was her husband, but then she was informed they would have to perform an emergency C-section on her, further exacerbating how she was feeling. When her attending physician informed her that they were going to have a medical intern join them in the delivery room, she was unable to refuse. Recalling the moment, she said, "I was so afraid. I truly could not speak. I'm telling you—I opened my mouth, but the words absolutely would not come out!" Her fear was paralyzing. She felt even more vulnerable and exposed in front of this perfect stranger. In an already stressful situation, the fond memory of the birth of Elle's child is clouded by a lack of awareness by the doctor, a lack of awareness that also made the memory a traumatizing one.

What can we actively do to build our hospitality muscles towards **all** the humans that we serve? Here are some examples from an article by Janice A. Sabin, PhD, MSW: "Actions that clinicians can take immediately to manage the effects of implicit bias include practicing conscious, positive formal and informal role modeling; taking active-bystander training to learn how to address or interrupt microaggressions and other harmful incidents; and undergoing training aimed at eliminating negative patient descriptions and stigmatizing words in chart notes and direct patient communications. Teaching faculty at academic medical centers can develop curricular materials that contain inclusive, diverse imagery and examples and can strive to use inclusive language in all written and oral communications."[30]

Our job in medicine is to help and heal, not to judge. A recent meme thankfully got a lot of pushback from the veterinary community when it showed a veterinarian whispering to a pet, "I am sorry your owners are idiots." Certainly, it is frustrating when people don't follow our advice or take advice from sketchy sources, but people are usually trying to do the best that they can with the information they are given. Our goal is to be their trusted advisor so that the education they receive is accurate and up-to-date but also affordable and doable. We can only do that by being curious and actively listening. People can feel when they are being judged. That is poor hospitality.

13

Serving Your Teammates Like Your Best Client

I remember the day I first walked into a veterinary practice.

It was 1985, and I was a young woman in a new town. I had a new apartment, a new job, and a husband in the same boat. We knew no one. I had been hired by Jean, the current office manager. She said that she had remembered me when I came to interview because of my "red winter coat and my blue eyes," which is funny because my eyes are green. Then, she made the connection between me and my family's barbecue restaurant where she would periodically travel to for dinner. I'm guessing that she received good customer service because she gave me a job. But that first day at work was very intimidating, even for someone like me who had grown up working with the public and surrounded by a crowd. At this point in time, the practice did not take appointments, so it was a poorly controlled free-for-all. The training was limited with the majority of it being "follow them." (In the training industry, "them" is anyone nearby who has a clue!) It was kind of a sink-or-swim environment.

That first day, I was introduced to the majority of the staff and shown how to file records and answer the telephone. To say it was overwhelming is an understatement. I made it through the first day and went home still excited about the possibilities but feeling less than competent while sharing animal medical stories with my husband. I was working for minimum wage, and I took the job just to get my foot in the door of animal health. I don't know that I would have stayed at that practice as long as I did or even for the first week if it wasn't for a grilled cheese sandwich.

My second day at work involved coming in and working the morning shift. It was then that I met Clara. Clara had been working at the practice for several years as a part-time morning receptionist. Her husband was an FBI agent, and she was a former flight attendant. Clara raised Borzois and Chesapeake Bay Retrievers, and she was one of the best customer service people I have ever met. But Clara's customer service went beyond taking care of clients because, that day, she also took care of me. I think she remembered what it was like to be a new person in town and to be the new person at work.

So, at lunch on my second day, Clara asked me to come to her house so that she could make me a grilled cheese sandwich. She lived close by in a beautiful home surrounded by pastures with high-wire fences so the sight hounds could run. We sat on bar stools at the kitchen counter drinking Diet Coke, eating our sandwiches, and getting to know each other. I have often looked back on Clara's generosity and random act of kindness as a linchpin in my career. She made me feel welcome. She invited me into her home and made me feel like I was not an outsider. Because of her kindness, I had a mentor and a new friend. I stayed at that practice for nineteen years. Clara had retired a couple of years prior to my leaving the practice to live closer to her kids, but we stayed in touch on Facebook.

I tell this story because we work so hard to hire talent in our practices, but then we neglect to make them feel welcome.

We bring them in and have them fill out paperwork, we reiterate the job description, we hand them the employee manual and tell them the rules, and, if they're lucky, we show them where to put their things and where the bathroom is. Onboarding a new person should be so much more than this. It should be a celebration of a new team member. They should be introduced to the team, taken out to lunch, and assigned a mentor and a trainer, and we should touch base daily to see how they are fitting in and what concerns they have.

The stats on great onboarding are impressive. New hires get up to speed and are productive much faster. They bond to the business and become engaged with the work, and, because they feel a part of something bigger than themselves, they STAY. It is impossible to build the culture you want and the skills your team needs with a revolving door of employees.

Have a PLAN for your new hires.

Often when we hire new staff members, they come to us fresh out of school or from another city. They know nothing about the area, housing, schools, and so on. As a hospitable employer, we can help. (See Appendix B for a sample new employee onboarding plan.)

I recently saw a social media post in which a manager wanted to develop a list for new hires of their favorite coffee drinks, food likes and dislikes, and preferences in entertainment or places to dine. I loved the idea because she wanted to get them things they loved as shout-outs for good performance. What would be even better is to manage by walking around and talking to people about themselves, not just about the work. What do they dream? How can you help make it come true? Leaders, pay attention to your people! Notice if they are struggling and offer a hand. Be there when they need you and encourage them to be there for each other.

There is an old manager adage called storming, norming, and forming. It is often used as an excuse to understand why the existing team, even though they might be suffering because they are shorthanded, will not embrace a new person and willingly help them get up to speed. Instead, they gaslight, bully, ostracize, and judge until the new person either quits or starts to fight back and settles in by becoming just as jaded as the rest of the group. This is insanity. Great leaders don't allow this, and they work to build a psychologically safe workplace. This is another reason why a mentor is so important to a new person. It gives them an ally in the "norming" part of the process and protects them in the "storming" part.

Of course, not every hire is a great fit, but every hire is a human being who deserves respect, kindness, and a chance to prove their ability to do the job. A culture of hospitality does this.

> **Every hire is a human being who deserves respect, kindness, and a chance to prove their ability to do the job.**

But what about the existing team? How can we improve the culture of our business when it seems overwhelming to change? How do we show hospitality to our coworkers?

In the current economy, there are more jobs than people to fill them.[31] Predictions show that all medical professions will be severely shorthanded in the very near future. By building a positive culture, we create a work environment of engaged staff that stay. Turnover has always been an issue in medicine, but there are practices that keep their team members for years. HOW? The answer is great culture and fair pay! You don't have to pay the top wages because people will willingly work for slightly less money as long as they enjoy coming to work and feel respected and valued there. But how do we know the truth about our culture and how our team perceives it?

To identify your culture, start with team surveys. Many practices find 360-degree reviews helpful to reveal problems. Reoccurring negative themes are signs that your team is feeling distressed by these issues. As a consultant, one of my first tasks is to perform one-on-one interviews with every staff member. I ask them how they feel about the practice, how they enjoy their coworkers and boss, and if they feel supported in their ambitions to grow in their career. We also do a "stop, start, and continue" exercise, which helps me find the operational processes that are working or lacking. I look for consistent themes from the group and usually find a few that everyone finds equally frustrating. There are many companies that offer 360-degree surveys; these surveys can be very helpful, but they must be used judiciously. If the team is not coached to be objective about the work performance they are reviewing, it can instead spiral into "mean girl"–type bashing and be more harmful than helpful, especially in a culture that needs improvement. Also, the person delivering the evaluations should review the content for biases and cliques and how they may negatively influence the feedback. If it is not going to be helpful and instead will cause emotional injury to the person being evaluated, then a judgment should be made about how to share feedback kindly, partially, or not at all.

As difficult as it is to hear negative feedback, it is vital to our personal growth and self-awareness.

In her book *Insight*, author Dr. Tasha Eurich shares the value of being self-aware when it comes to being successful in all human interactions.[32] Repeatedly, leaders feel that they are doing a wonderful job. They are positive that they are admired and respected by their team, but when finding out that they are, instead, considered a person to be feared and avoided, they are shocked.

No one sets out with intention to be a bad boss, manager, or team member, but in some cases, our personality style and mistaken beliefs about how people should be treated and how work gets done create a monster. This ogre is causing a distinct lack of production by the team as they operate not to do great work but, instead, to not get raked over the coals for errors large or small, real, or perceived. On the opposite side of the coin is the boss who can't make a decision or confront a problematic employee who is undermining the success of the team because they fear and avoid conflict. Both leaders are equally unaware of how they are viewed by their subordinates and how much damage they are doing to the group.

Research shows that self-aware people are more successful, confident, and fulfilled.[31] They are more effective leaders. Yet most people don't truly know themselves or see themselves as others see them. In a presentation I attended by Dr. Eurich, she asked, "How many of you consider yourself a good driver?" Of course, most of the people in the room quickly raised their hands. Then, she asked, "How many of you think most people can't drive?" An equal number of audience members raised their hands. Laughingly, she said, "Do you see the problem here? Many of you are the bad drivers, yet all of you think you drive well. That is lack of self-awareness." If you are interested in learning more about your own self-awareness, Dr. Eurich offers a free quiz on her website at https://www.insight-book.com/Quiz.

Turnover is another sign of poor cultural health. How often are you placing ads for staff? I have known a practice that never removed their help-wanted ads from trade journals. Having visited the practice, I understood the reason for the need. The owner's wife was the manager and micromanaged everything and everyone. It was a stifling environment in which to work.

Other signs of poor culture are chronic absences by staff, unwillingness to step up to occasionally cover shifts for coworkers, and being locked into the letter of job descriptions. When I share that I used to allow my team to trade days off or arrange their own schedules without my approval, many managers are stunned. The rules were simple. You could trade with anyone who had equal skills and who, if you swapped, would not get overtime in that week. I did monitor the system for fairness because I didn't want people to be taken advantage of who were so kind that they never said "no." People appreciated my trust in them to make good decisions, and they liked the autonomy of making their own plans. I felt that I had hired responsible adults, and they were treated as such unless they proved otherwise. Granted, most of my team members were long-time employees, and their actions had earned them the privilege to trade with their coworkers.

We must certainly add gossip and drama to the bad-culture list. Good communication training solves many of these issues. In fact, learning about personality styles is one of the most drama-reducing skills I teach. But some people have developed a deeply ingrained habit of negativity, fault finding, and pot stirring and, even after appropriate coaching, do not work to change. In fact, they routinely blame everyone besides themselves for the problems. Remember the discussion about lack of self-awareness? These folks are the poster children. Sometimes removing these toxic staff members can be painful, especially if they are one of your most technically skilled people.

I remember well how difficult this was when I was a manager. I fired a very reliable, hardworking person for gossiping. She just couldn't break this bad habit and continually caused drama by pot stirring. I dismissed a tech with twenty years of experience because of her passive-aggressive actions. She would hide instruments, charts, and other items in what she deemed was "her" drawer. Everyone was afraid to go into the drawer because of her prickly demeanor. When I found out about this, I opened that drawer and found all our missing items. The wheels immediately went into motion to move her out. The day I released her was the best day ever. The entire team felt like a heavy burden had been lifted off their backs. The toxic tension in the treatment room dissipated. The remaining staff stepped up to cover the workload. It was amazing how the very air in the room seemed charged with positive energy after she was gone.

> **As hard as it is, you must release the people on your team that are undermining your success.**

How do you repair a broken culture?

First, define the culture that you desire. Create a set of core values for the whole team—including practice owners—to live by, as mentioned earlier. People who do not agree with or believe in the same core values as defined by the practice are not good fits and need to be released to grow elsewhere. As an example, if you have a high-end practice and one of your staff members does not support your fee structure because they feel that it is too expensive, then they are not advocating for the level of care that you provide. Their perception of value will also come across to your clients as they interact with them.

Second, purge toxic team members. Owners and managers are surprised at the stories shared after these people are fired. To start, determine if the toxic employee can be saved—because humans tend to avoid giving negative feedback until they are angry. Perhaps the employee has not had the opportunity to improve their behavior. Set deadlines for touching base. Have frequent feedback sessions. Find out if the employee's career goals are being met. If not, what can you do to help them accomplish their goals? Always try coaching for improvement first, and if that fails, release the employee. People who refuse to see themselves truthfully will not comply and will fire themselves with their refusal to change.

Third, train the staff to well-defined job descriptions. Frustration runs rampant in staff that is unsure of the job and how to perform it correctly. Phase training documents are essential for complete and thorough training of the staff. Basically, these checklists confirm that all the important skills of the job have been taught and both the trainee and trainer are comfortable with the knowledge that has been passed along. In addition, develop levels; as the trainee passes each level, they reach a new "status" and pay grade. Upward mobility can be achieved.

> **"The only thing worse than training employees and losing them is not training them and keeping them."**
> —Zig Ziglar

Fourth, choose wisely. "Hire slow and fire fast" is a time-worn adage, but it holds true. My audiences are often shocked when I share that I fired new hires after only two weeks once I realized that they were a poor fit for our work team. This accomplished several things. The new hire had the opportunity to accept other recent offers, which would have been filled if I had waited longer. My team was not wasting valuable time training a bad hire, and the culture was not disrupted by a person who would never fit in. In this decision, I was respectful of all the stakeholders needs and quickly corrected my mistake. Using better screening and behavior-based interview questions and calling references are all important parts of picking your next superstar employee. Don't go on gut—go on fact. Get other team members involved in the hiring process during work interviews. If they are engaged in picking the new person, there is greater chance that they will support and embrace them.

> **When hiring, don't go on gut—go on fact.**

Fifth, allow autonomy in your team. Personal growth and the practice's commitment to encourage career advancement improve culture. Multiple surveys support the importance of these features. People leave jobs when they feel stagnant. I recommend having job proficiency levels paired with pay grades. Level 1 includes new hires who still need to learn the basics. Level 2 employees have mastered the basics and move up to learning and mastering more complex responsibilities. Level 3 employees have achieved mastery of all the levels of skills and are qualified to train others. Level 4 is the master trainer who enjoys teaching and is highly proficient. By creating pay grades and levels based on skills, we allow people to move up, so they don't have to move out. Employees need to see a bright future with your business, especially if they have ambitions to achieve a higher rank. Another advancement opportunity is delegating specific functions to interested staff members. Delegating tasks to staff members not only gives them encouragement to grow but also takes a lot of the burden off of owners and managers, freeing them up for strategic planning and prac-tice development. Delegating is a good way to reward your high-level staff when they have reached your highest pay grade. Owning and performing a new task well is another reason to bump pay. Don't dump tasks on people without first asking if they are interested in the project, and never assign someone more work without increasing their compensation. That is unfair and highly demotivating. Delegate, but always check back. Don't abandon people with a new task until you are sure that they are comfortable and doing it correctly. (See Appendix B for the steps of successful delegation.)

We discussed self-awareness and empowerment, but let's look at the hospitality factor of kindness. Are we being truly kind to one another as we work together to help our patients? In Christine Porath and Christine Pearson's *The Cost of Bad Behavior*, astonishing amounts of money were found to be lost each year from companies just because the staff was ill-treated by others—often management—who lead by fear rather than by positive reinforcement and kind corrections.[33] These "bad behaviors" may seem minor, as one of the listed problems was "coming in and not speaking to coworkers." Does a simple "good morning" require so much effort that you instead rudely ignore your teammates? There is truly no excuse unless you have laryngitis, and even then, you can wave! Manners are usually taught in childhood, but it is possible that some people have not had good training. If so, leaders should coach these team members on better behavior because their apparent rudeness is causing a rift and creating workplace stress. Leaders should also set the example. I remember walking down the hall one day, and as I passed my boss, he asked rather gruffly, "What are you smiling about?" I grinned and responded, "Lack of damn sense, I guess!" This made him laugh, shake his head, and walk on. I was smiling because I enjoyed my clients, my teammates, my work, and, of course, the animals. What was there not to smile about?

I can't stress the importance of how a lack of civility destroys culture and productivity in a business. Some of the actions that Porath and Pearson mention in *The Cost of Bad Behavior* are taking credit for others' work, texting or checking emails while in meetings, passing blame for personal mistakes on to others, belittling others' efforts, spreading rumors about teammates, failing to reply to calls or emails, not saying "please" or "thank you," leaving a mess for others to clean, not listening, talking down to others, making demeaning or derogatory remarks to others, and taking or hiding resources[34] (remember the story about the drawer). All these actions may seem minor but, added up, can rapidly eat holes in the fabric of a positive culture. Speaker Amy Newfield recently posted a video on Facebook called "Stop Throwing Instruments!" I have heard too many stories of doctors having meltdowns and, in a fit of temper, throwing surgical instruments either on the floor or at their attending nurse. This is, to me, a fireable offense. The problem comes when it is the practice owner who is the culprit. Once again, we need to step back to the self-awareness discussion and give feedback to the offender.

When I began my last position as the chief operating officer of a large veterinary practice, there was an assistant who was known to have temper tantrums and storm out of the building in a fit of rage. This happened around my fourth day at work. I called her into a private area and explained that her behavior was understandable because I was a new leader and everyone was a little tense, waiting to see how I would behave. I said, "Tiffany, I am going to give you this one because I know everyone is on edge, but in the future, please know that this behavior will not be tolerated." If you can't control your emotions, and if you pitch a fit and storm out the door, you will no longer be employed by this practice." I did not raise my voice or become angry. I just calmly stated the behavior that I expected from an adult. She never did it again.

When discussing this type of negative behavior, I sometimes have people push back with "sometimes you can't control it" to which I reply, "Nonsense! If you got angry at a stranger and began to verbally abuse them, and they pulled out a knife or a gun, I guarantee that you would immediately gain control of your mouth." You understand that it is in your best interest to shut up so that you don't die. Learning to control your behavior is one of the key elements of a successful career and an enjoyable life. People who fly off the handle do not get promoted, or at least they shouldn't be because they can't be trusted by their team. Words hurt us mentally and are remembered long after the memory of physical pain leaves us. Not only is incivility a productivity killer, but ninety-four percent of people treated this way work to get even with their offenders.[35] So if you are one of the people who feels that it is okay to treat others badly, watch your back, and if you are an employer who allows this behavior, eighty-eight percent of employees also work to get even with their company! Consider the number of mass shootings that occur in the workplace. Here are some eye-opening data from the FBI: "Of 160 active-shooter incidents in the

United States between 2000 and 2013, over 80 percent (132) occurred at work .... Of the 132 work-site shootings, seventy-three incidents (45.6 percent) took place at businesses. The seventy-three incidents that occurred in business environments resulted in 210 people killed (including twelve company owners, supervisors, or managers) and 272 people wounded (including six owners, supervisors or managers) .... Thirty-four shooters were employed or previously employed by the business, including twenty-two current employees, seven former employees, four terminated on the day of the shooting, and one suspended employee."[36] I certainly don't want to imply that if you don't behave kindly to your coworkers that they will intend to do you physical harm, but I do believe that treating people with respect and learning conflict resolution and communication skills could solve many of the problems we have with stress, burnout, poor productivity, and turnover.

To build a great team you must communicate well and often. Well-planned staff meetings are a bridge between the practice owner's goals and the team's understanding of them. They are also an opportunity to share information from different views. At a minimum, a practice should hold monthly team meetings, but quickly huddling every morning and afternoon is a great way to keep everyone in the loop. As the chief operating officer of a twenty-four-hour practice, it was challenging to have all-hands-on-deck meetings, but we made a point to hold them at least twice a year. Instead, every month we held department meetings, with the department heads of all departments attending each separate group's meeting. The idea was to ensure interdepartmental information flow. Then, the department leaders could be there to help find solutions to communication gaps and take the solutions back to their team. We don't need everyone at every meeting, but we do need everyone to stay informed about challenges and changes that affect them and their work. The meeting dates were posted in January for the entire year, and they rotated being held on Tuesday, Wednesday, or Thursday so that staff members who had regular days off did not have to always come in during their valuable downtime to attend. Minutes were also taken and posted so all could read and reference back to the discussions.

Meetings are frequently seen as a huge waste of time by employees. They are if not done correctly. Agendas should be posted at least a week in advance so that the staff can have time to contemplate the issues and consider ideas for solutions. The meetings should allow all attendees time to speak and avoid the "conversation hog" taking over the discussion. The facilitator has this duty. In addition to solving any problems the business has encountered, there should be a learning component where all are taught a new skill, share insights from a book, learn lessons from a podcast or a TED talk, receive training from an outside speaker on a new product, or are shown a new life skill.

Finally, the group needs to set goals for the month. These could be productivity goals, but even more important are communication goals and client service innovations that help bond clients to the team and the business. We should also review how the prior month's goals were met and diagnose failures and successes. The reason why people hate meetings is that they are poorly planned and like a dog chasing its tail: they often end in frustration rather than progress.

All agree that gaining client trust is a big part of successfully treating our patients and getting to "yes." But just as important is the trust our team has in their leadership and in each other.

We want to know that we have one another's backs—not that we are likely to stab one another in the back. When team members feel safe, they will self-monitor rather than bring every minor thing to the manager to solve.

I was in a recent practice visit working with the CSR team. These were some talented people. I could tell by their responses to my questions that they were great at problem-solving, bonding with clients, and building relationships. But their complaint was that "no one ever acknowledges our work or gives us a compliment on how we handle the front desk." So, I turned it back on them and asked, "When was the last time you gave a compliment to one another? Who said you can't give feedback and support to yourselves?" They seemed surprised and then delighted because they could see that they could be the change they wanted to see.

I wouldn't be surprised if, when they follow through on this support of one another, the other departments will start to observe and want what they have. They could be the model of a safe and kind culture to the rest of the team. The hospitality approach to work builds supportive and caring teams that stay.

A long time ago I learned about Maslow's hierarchy of human needs. It begins at the bottom—food, water, air—which is about as fundamental as you can get. Then, the next step is safety, which is embodied by security of body, employment, resources, morality, and health. You can easily see that when a business can't or won't meet the second, most basic need of a human—SAFETY—none of the other desires can happen.

You can't build belonging in a team when there is no trust. You can't gain the confidence and self-esteem needed to garner respect for yourself and for others if you are never safe. And you certainly can't grow to the transformative stage of self-actualization, where creativity and problem-solving flourish, when you are always afraid.

Great culture moves teams to the pinnacle of the hierarchy. Staff members are enveloped in such safety that they bond in friendships. Don't feel like coming to work? If I don't, I let my friends down ... so I will come. Want to feel a sense of belonging? Then I will pitch in and help when my work team is performing a task. Want to be respected by the people I work with? Then I will stretch myself to come up to their belief in me and meet their high expectations.

Great culture is not that hard—it is about choosing wisely the people who believe what you believe, who understand the why of our work. It is about hiring those who desire to be a part of something important in the world and then nurturing their core values with support, feedback, and kindness while protecting them from harm.

> **Great culture is about choosing wisely the people who believe what you believe, who understand the why of our work.**

I always believed that a significant part of my job as a manager was to protect my people. So, I took the heat from the difficult client. I was the go-between for my super-driver-personality boss and my staff. I found ways to teach them so that they would have confidence. I confessed my mistakes to them so that they felt free to come and confess theirs. I fired people who didn't perform. Leaders drive the culture, and great culture drives successful business, just as poor culture tears it down.

As we hire a young generation that does not believe in loyalty for the sake of loyalty, creating a positive culture that grows, supports, and engages staff members becomes essential for practice success. "My way or the highway" has never been a good management philosophy and becomes even more archaic in today's hiring environment. **Team members want to know that their leaders are working for a meaningful purpose and that these leaders are committed to guiding their team members to career success. Pick them well, train them hard, grow them fast, give them power—and love them lots.** You are going to like what happens.

The moral of the story is never waste a chance to share a grilled cheese. It set my career in motion, and thirty-five years later, I still smile about that lunch at Clara's.

EXERCISE: Consider the new employees on your team. What random act of kindness did you perform to make them feel welcome? What could you have done if you did nothing? What will you do to welcome the next new hire?

14

Conflict Happens: How to Successfully Navigate Difficult Encounters

As much as we would like to build a culture that never has drama, we are always working with humans who are imperfect and emotion-driven, so conflict will arise. The important and often missing piece of the puzzle is understanding the cause of conflict and teaching the team how to move into conflict correctly rather than avoiding it and allowing problems to fester until they explode.

Humans naturally avoid uncomfortable situations. They delay action until they are pressed to the point of extreme frustration and are forced to act. For some people, this point is much closer than for others who are more tolerant and laid back. For either, when that tipping point is reached, the "smart brain" that makes wise judgments has typically been hijacked by the "lizard brain" that reacts to fear. Let me share some brain science that will help clarify.

Our brain is typically broken down into three parts. The lizard brain, which is our brain stem, is the most primitive part of the brain; thus, it has the name "lizard brain" because we react like a reptile to stimuli. It controls most of the body's vital functions—like breathing, heart rate, sleeping, and waking—and it never rests (at least you hope it doesn't because you are going to die if it does). The lizard brain is also referred to as the limbic brain, and it is designed to keep us from harm and keep our body functioning at the most basic level. Neuroscientists say it controls the four Fs: fighting, feeding, fleeing, and *reproduction* (you can supply the fourth "F" on your own).

The paleomammalian brain is the part of the brain that sits on top of the brain stem. The amygdala is the part of this area of the brain that allows us to feel rage, pleasure, and fear and stores memories of those emotions. The hippocampus converts short-term memories to long-term memories, and the thalamus connects the senses, sending signals throughout the brain. The cortex is highly specialized, with sections for vision, speech, and memory.

The cerebrum is the third part and sits at the front part of the brain. It is the largest part of the brain and allows us to coordinate our movements, regulate our body temperature, speak, think, create art, reason, solve problems, develop emotions, and learn. Also associated with the cerebrum are vision, hearing, touch, taste, and smell.

Why does all this matter when discussing conflict?

Because when we were evolving, so were our brains. We learned that in order to survive around animals much larger and stronger than us, the best solution was teamwork. If you wanted to eat a wooly mammoth, you were going to starve or die if you tried killing it by yourself. Instead, you got together with others in your tribe and figured out a strategy. Humans are wired to collaborate. This is one of the reasons why we were so distressed in isolation during the COVID-19 pandemic. Our ability to be with others was severely curtailed, and it took an emotional toll on our collective mental health.

Humans have something that no other animal has; it is called "theory of mind." We attempt to see our world in terms of what motivates others' actions, and we try to predict another person's mental state. Are they happy, sad, angry, or calm? What were their intentions behind an action? Do they mean to help us or harm us? These judgments are an important part of our social structure. When we empathize with others, we are using theory of mind to "feel how they feel" by putting ourselves in their shoes. People who are good at reading the emotions of others and their own emotions are said to be emotionally intelligent. In the book *Emotional Intelligence 2.0* by Travis Bradberry and Jean Graves, the authors share a surprising finding. People with high IQs outperform people with average IQs only twenty percent of the time.[37] So being blessed with traditional intelligence is not a sure path to a successful life. However, people with high emotional intelligence and average IQs outperform high-IQ people **seventy percent of the time**. The conclusion is that emotional intelligence tops "book smarts" almost every time.

When we lack emotional intelligence, instead of working collaboratively with people, we cause them to mentally move from safety to fear, greatly reducing their performance. We also exacerbate situations with clients who are unhappy.

Why? Because in a fearful state, the paleomammalian brain is flooded with stress hormones. The hypothalamus signals the adrenals to dump adrenaline into your body to prepare to flee or fight. Our bodies evolved to react in seconds, so our hormones move fast. When the danger is perceived as over, cortisol shows up and calms us back down.[38]

This is truly oversimplified, but you get the picture. When you are frightened or angry, you can't learn, think, or perform to your best standards. Stress like this over time causes something called "learned helplessness." Social workers and psychologists see this behavior in an abused spouse or even in some staff members who are victimized by bullies on their team. This could certainly explain why these abused workers simply don't quit.

According to Dr. John Medina, author of *Brain Rules*, our brain at work and our brain at home can't be separated.[39] If we are living under a chronically stressed state, such as with an abusive spouse or parent, our brain becomes exhausted because it feels that it has no control over this terrible situation. Our hypothalamus dumps adrenaline into our system at the instant in which we perceive a threat to our life. During evolution, these threats were short-lived, like encountering a snake in the yard. Your brain signals danger, and you freeze in place with your heart pounding. The blood is pumping oxygen to all your limbs so you can flee the snake. Once it moves on, the human body responds by immediately calming down, and sometimes we can even feel slightly "deflated" as we relax, realizing the danger is over. Then, we go about our normal day.

When people are constantly subjected to abuse, the fear is never-ending, and the spikes of adrenaline happen multiple times a day, never giving the body a time to calm and rest. The spikes can even come *in anticipation* of abuse because of the memory of past incidents. Physically, this can lead to a heart attack or stroke because the heart-pumping reaction scars the blood vessels. Cortisol also damages the hippocampus, causing the victim of abuse to be unable to learn or remember. Keep in mind that this is not only limited to physical abuse but can also apply to verbal abuse. Memories of physical and emotional pain are stored in the same area of the brain.

In the book *The Cost of Bad Behavior*, the authors discuss how incivility at work harms employee health by sharing the Harvard University School of Public Health study information that concluded that stressful jobs were as detrimental to women's health as smoking and obesity.[40] A *Harvard Business Review* article notes the following: "The American Psychological Association estimates that more than $500 billion is siphoned off from the U.S. economy because of workplace stress, and 550 million workdays are lost each year due to stress on the job. Sixty percent to 80 percent of workplace accidents are attributed to stress, and it's estimated that more than 80 percent of doctor visits are due to stress."[41] The article additionally highlights the following: "In studies by the Queens School of Business and by the Gallup Organization, disengaged workers had 37 percent higher absenteeism, 49 percent more accidents, and 60 percent more errors and defects. In organizations with low employee engagement scores, they experienced 18 percent lower productivity, 16 percent lower profitability, 37 percent lower job growth, and 65 percent lower share price over time. Importantly, businesses with highly engaged employees enjoyed 100 percent more job applications."[41]

Consider how workplace stress can affect patient care if we are facing a sixty percent increase in errors and defects in organizations with negative workplace cultures. Over the years, I have listened to multiple stories of cultures so deep in conflict that team members will allow a doctor to make a mistake that harms a patient without intervening because they are afraid of the repercussions of speaking up or retaliation for perceived harms. It is inappropriate for us to fear our coworkers and superiors, and it is poor leadership that tolerates behavior that creates such fear.

The takeaway of this information is to keep your team "feeling safe" if you want them to learn, grow, and achieve high performance and have faith that calling out an error will be applauded rather than cursed.

> **Keep your team "feeling safe" if you want them to learn, grow, and achieve high performance.**

How do you confront someone with necessary but negative feedback in a way that allows them to not only accept it but to also use it to make positive changes to avoid similar mistakes moving forward? The answer is to approach the problem with your "smart brain" and use curiosity rather than accusations.

When we approach someone with a statement like "You are always late to work," we are stating a false fact if that person is late only two days a week. They immediately become defensive and contradict your statement by saying, "That is not true. I am on-time almost every day." A better approach would be to say, "Toni, I see that you were late to work by twenty minutes on Tuesday and twenty-seven minutes on Friday. Can you share with me what is going on in your life that is causing you to be late to work?" The tone of the sentence has moved from an accusation of slack work habits to a concern something disruptive is happening to make this person late. The need for Toni to defend herself is gone, and an opening is given for a reasonable explanation.

For many years, I have sung the praises of the book *Crucial Conversations*,[42] touting it as my "bible for communication and conflict training." This book has more dog-eared pages and highlights than any other book on my shelves. The authors define these tough conversations as times when the participants have differing opinions, the outcome matters significantly to both parties, and highly emotional responses are manifesting on both sides. Many of our conflicts in the medical field are high-stakes discussions with the decision maker sitting on the fence between accepting the medical care we offer and understanding its value to their lives or accusing us of everything from price gouging to malpractice. The emotions in these types of conversations are powerful on both sides with the medical team feeling accused of horrible behavior far from their sworn oath and the client or patient feeling taken advantage of at a most vulnerable time when they or their beloved pet is ill. Learning how to navigate these conversations not only improves the outcome for the patient but also avoids the unnecessary stress of constant scolding by the public.

Remember that our limbic (lizard) brain is wired to react in milliseconds to threats of perceived danger. It moves through the freeze, flee, and fight response and quickly takes over our normal, cool intellect if we don't train ourselves to stop, breathe, and engage our higher-level thinking.

For me, visualization is helpful. I think of myself as a long camera lens. When engaged with a person in normal conversations, I am focused at a "close-up" level. If the conversation turns to conflict, I try to pull my "lens focus" back to a wide-angle view to take in the broader aspects of what is happening. I work to diagnose the situation, asking myself the following questions: "What is this person feeling? How did I miscommunicate to set this conflict in motion? Why do they feel like they need to defend themselves? Where did their fear or feeling of disrespect originate? What can I say to de-escalate this conversation?" I also give myself an internal pep talk, with language like, "This is not about you but rather something they perceive that you or the practice did to them. This is a challenge you enjoy. I can turn this conversation around with my skills. Just ride along and listen."

Notice that I removed my emotional response from the process, which allowed me to be objective about the situation. This does take practice and a lot of self-control, but it is a skill that should be honed. Not only does it work for difficult client or team member interactions, but the same skill can also be used at home with your family.

Another tool in these conversations is to find a common goal with your conversation partner. Why is this person in your office? Is it because they want to find a solution to a medical issue that is causing them distress or to help their pet who is ill? Because we are medical professionals, our goal is to heal and help; therefore, we are working towards the same objective as our client.

Human nature demands us to do the exact opposite of what I have described. Our limbic brain wants us to scamper away from these challenging conversations, avoiding confrontation at all costs, or wants us to attack our accuser, prove ourselves right, and WIN! If we can keep in mind that this is a negotiation and not a battle, we are more likely to come away with a compromise that both sides can live with.

Returning to a prior discussion of active listening, this is a vital tool in a difficult conversation, especially when the person you are speaking with seems to be pulling issues out of some make-believe universe visible only to them. In his book *Talking to Crazy: How to Deal with the Irrational and Impossible People in Your Life*, Dr. Mark Goulston gives us advice on managing those people who appear to be completely off the rails. He describes four irrational behaviors. First, they can't see the world clearly. Second, they make no sense in what they say or think. Third, they do things in opposition to their own best interest. Finally, they refuse to be guided to reason. For example, what rational person believes they will get better care by shouting at and disrespecting their medical caregiver? Or get better service from their waiter? Or have a loving relationship with their kids? None of these actions is logical, but the "lizard brain" defies logic.

Dr. Goulston's advice is to "lean in to crazy" to change the situation's dynamic. I used this tactic recently when attempting to buy a dog. I had searched for two years for a small fuzzy dog and, thanks to a friend, made a connection with a breeder who had a fourteen-month-old, retired champion Bichon Frise. In my estimation, this dog was old enough to not have to go through the up-every-two-hours puppy stage, had been well socialized because of the show ring and living at his handler's home with three kids and eight dogs, and came with three generations of health testing for genetic issues and proved sound. I began an email conversation with the breeder and, because of my long history in veterinary medicine, began to ask what I considered to be a lot of reasonable questions about behavior, health, medical care, and obedience training. Apparently, the breeder took these questions to be a personal affront to the quality of her dogs and her skill as a breeder. She was close to the point of refusing to sell me the dog. Finally, I texted her a message of apology, stating that the miscommunication was all my fault and that if I had started my dog project by first visiting her website, where many of my questions would have been answered, she would not believe that I questioned her commitment to her dogs. I explained that the only reason I shared my experience in veterinary medicine and animal behavior was to show her that the dog would have exceptional care at my home, which was our mutual goal. So, it all worked out, and I adore my new pup and frequently text his breeder pictures to keep her up to date. I simply realized that I was going to need to "lean in to crazy" to work through the communication with her.

Thinking back, I believe several things were going on. This lady really loves her dogs, and giving up a dog you raised and had for fourteen months would be difficult, especially to a stranger you had never met. Perhaps she had been bashed by someone in the veterinary community for breeding dogs, even though her regular veterinarian turned out to be a personal friend of mine and shared that she was an excellent owner. Quality preservationist breeders, who work to improve the genetic health of their breed, are often dumped in the same basket as the "backyard" breeder, who just wants to profit from the sale of animals. Having experienced both, I can assure you that there is a difference. So, giving her some grace and being willing to not have to prove myself right got me a wonderful pet.

Some people set out to make you crazy. They make snide remarks and little jabs about things that matter to you and hope to get a rise and negative reaction from you in return. Don't play their game. I used to have clients that made remarks about how expensive our care was for their pets. Rather than getting defensive, I just said, "In my experience, you get what you pay for, and quality care costs. But I really appreciate your business because, without you, I wouldn't have a job, and I really love my job! Besides, look how happy your pet looks. You are a great pet owner, and I wish everyone took as good of care of their pet as you do." Of course, this was not how they expected me to reply, and it completely threw them off their game. It was said in a playful manner and with a smile, but it was also said in seriousness and with a belief in our quality of care.

In all conflicts, assume positive intent. I found that my most helpful tools going into these challenging encounters were a pen, a pad of paper, and a few deep breaths. I would ask the client to start at the beginning and share their story while taking notes about *what they believed* had occurred. I never contradicted or corrected their story for accuracy. I continued to nod, take notes, and ask clarifying questions. I discovered that allowing the client to tell their story from their perspective without argument or interruption gave them the opportunity to get their frustrations and anger out and finally wind down to an emotional state that I could reason with. Before they got to that calmer state, there was no point in sharing my side because they were in amygdala hijack, and the logical part of their brain was not engaged, just the primitive limbic brain that believed it was fighting for its survival. Many people don't have the patience to wait until the end of the story; instead, they interrupt to attempt to tell their side. This only makes the client dig in harder because they don't believe that you are listening. I once had a disgruntled client tell me that he felt like he had to go to battle every time he came into the practice because of the poor customer service he encountered. I had been hired to change this issue a few weeks earlier and, thankfully, managed to do so in the months ahead. When I asked him why he kept returning, he replied, "Because these are the best veterinarians in the area, and I want them to care for my pets." Even then, the poor hospitality he was receiving could have eventually driven him away.

> **Once you get people to a calmer state, it is time to develop an allyship with them and help them fight for their cause.**

Thank people for complaining! Usually, there is a kernel of truth in even the most elaborate story. I always said to upset people, "Thank you for telling me about this because if I don't know, I can't fix it. I didn't want this to happen to you, and I really don't want to have it happen to others! I truly appreciate your feedback." It was typical for the complaining person to apologize for their behavior after we finished our conversation.

Never tell people to "calm down" or that they "can't seriously believe that is true" because you are not going to get through to them. You are only pouring fuel on the fire.

According to the book *Emotional Intelligence 2.0*, humans have five basic emotions: happy, sad, angry, afraid, and ashamed.[43] The Gottman Institute has six emotions: mad, scared, joyful, powerful, peaceful, and sad.[44] Both resources break down these basic emotions into more incremental intensity levels. For example, "mad" can be deconstructed into hurt, hostile, angry, rage, hateful, and critical at the medium-intensity level, but those then move into jealous, selfish, frustrated, furious, irritated, and skeptical at mild intensity. So, when my CSR used to come to me with a request to talk with Mrs. Smith who was MAD, I typically discovered that the client was in a milder state of frustration or irritation.

People are typically not very good at defining their emotions. I find that doctors in particular classify their reactions to an accuser as angry, when it is really about feeling disrespected about their skills and knowledge.

Sometimes they are also uneasy about the fact that there may be a word of truth in what they are being told. Imposter syndrome kicks in and confidence diminishes. We begin to tell ourselves a false story. Here is a very important brain fact that you need to keep at the forefront of your mind: THE BRAIN DOES NOT KNOW THE TRUTH FROM A LIE ... IT ONLY KNOWS WHAT YOU TELL IT.

When we feed our brain negativity, it seeks to find more of that to affirm our belief as a truth. For example, you believe that a fellow staff member doesn't care for you. You have never had a real conflict, but maybe one day in the treatment room, she gave you a sharp remark. Now your brain tries to mind read, and because you have told it that this girl doesn't like you, it looks for anything she does that confirms your belief. Even her most innocent remarks are perceived by your brain as hurtful. We allow this story to continue if we don't become the master of our emotions and talk to ourselves, saying, "Why would this person not like me? Perhaps that day she was very pushed and busy, and that is why she made that remark. Let me go and speak with her to clear this up." That is a grown-up thought process. Author and speaker Brené Brown has a great line for these situations: "The story I am telling myself about this situation is this ... Now, can you please tell me how you see it?" This line should be in our employee manual!

The good news is that communication skills and emotional intelligence can be learned. As people age, they typically gain better emotional skills because they discover that what they did in the past didn't work effectively. Humans learn by failure. Fortunately, the books I have referenced, and many similar titles, can help you avoid the need to fail in order to improve because we can learn from others' mistakes by reading. I certainly wouldn't manage a difficult client interaction today the same way I did at age twenty-five. At the time, I was a new practice manager. I recall explaining an exam fee to a client, and when she complained about being charged the fee for her dog who had received a steroid injection, I said, "Lady, I won't kill your dog for twenty dollars, and, if you want me to, you need to go someplace else for vet care." Then, I copied her dog's one-page paper record and slid it across the counter. Please don't do that! Use your hospitality skills to do a much better job.

> **EXERCISE:** Think of a time when you told yourself a false story about a coworker or a friend. What effect did it have on your relationship? What happened when you discovered your mistake?

15

The Importance of Language in Discussing Money

Medical professionals and their team members are typically not trained in sales, so having to discuss financial matters with a client is considered to be the most uncomfortable conversation in practice. However, clients want us to be up-front about costs and to also have systems in place that aid them in affording care when necessary.

Our culture has trained us to be secretive about money. We are told not to discuss our salary and not to ask what an item costs or how much someone paid for their home. The downside of all this is that we can be taken advantage of by a boss who is underpaying us in comparison to another employee at the same level, or we go to buy the item that our friend has purchased only to find it unaffordable. We don't know how to negotiate for a home because we have no point of reference as to what someone else recently paid for a home of similar size and age in the same neighborhood on the same street. In recent years, technology has pulled back the curtain on many of these money secrets by posting salaries and home prices online.

Healthcare costs, however, are still held in mystery. Occasionally, a veterinary hospital will post fees for routine care like vaccinations, exams, or neutering, but by far, the majority of vet practices don't. In fact, they are so secretive about fees that they won't even answer these questions when clients call or email. All this cloak-and-dagger activity leads to a lack of trust and results in clients being surprised by costs once they're in the clinic.

Human patients with health insurance usually have an idea of their co-pays and deductibles, but because human health insurance pays the medical provider directly, the patient rarely has an idea of what the cost of care is for their own health services. As a cancer survivor, I used to review my explanation of benefits and be stunned at the cost of care compared to similar products or procedures in veterinary medicine. Even with insurance, the co-pays became significant, and I was thankful that my hospital had a system in place for payments. I also had the benefit of supplemental insurance.

Pet insurance is different than human health insurance. It works similar to property insurance. Clients must pay the provider out of pocket and then submit their claim to be reimbursed. Therefore, the challenge is how to help a client bridge the gap between the time of care and the time of reimbursement. Practices must have tools in place to be able to work with their clients on finances. Otherwise, pets who could be saved will be subject to economic euthanasia. Not only does the pet lose but so does the pet owner and the animal health team that came into the profession to heal animals, not euthanize them.

Veterinary staff members assume that pet owners don't want to pay for care. A provider may think they can make judgments about who can and will pay and who won't. In my experience, that is an impossible call.

> **We can never assume the extent to which people love their animals and neither can we X-ray their bank account to know if they can afford the care we offer.**

Doing so is arrogant. Some people can afford the gold-standard level of care yet still not be willing to pay for it, while others may struggle to pay yet desperately want the best for their pet. Having worked the front desk for many years, I saw this play out many times.

Practices must address costs and prepare clients for the expenses they will incur as responsible pet owners. In several recent studies, the lifetime cost of a pet was evaluated. The lifetime cost of caring for dogs ranges from $20,000 to $55,000 and $15,000 to $45,000 for cats, according to the Synchrony 2021 Pet Lifetime of Care study. The study found that seven out of ten pet owners said they consider their pets as members of the family, yet nearly half underestimated the lifetime cost of caring for pets. The Lifetime of Care research also revealed that dog owners can expect to spend between $1,300 and $2,800 and cat owners, approximately $960 to $2,500 in the first year alone. One out of four pet owners surveyed indicated an unexpected expense of only $250 would cause them stress.[45] Not only does this relatively small amount of money cause owners distress, but they also are woefully uninformed about the real costs involved in maintaining the health of their furry family members. In the Pet Owners Economic Value Study by the Veterinary Hospital Managers Association, when asked what a preferred cost of a pet's dental cleaning should be, the respondents shared a price of sixty-five to ninety dollars, which is much lower than the typical average anesthesia-based dentistry cost of $500 to $900.[46]

> **Education about care costs should start at the initial visit with information provided about what to do to keep pets healthy and the anticipated costs as the pet ages.**

I used to give new pet owners a brochure that explained preventive care from puppyhood and the kitten stage to adulthood, then to the senior stage, and, finally, to the geriatric stage. The message was reinforced as the pet aged, and when the animal reached senior status, the extra diagnostics and exams were not a surprise. The one constant challenge that will certainly start conflict is blindsiding a client about costs. There are options for client financing, such as the CareCredit® health and pet care credit card—that I recommend practices should always accept—along with traditional credit cards, split billing, and auto drafting options. We can even provide piecemeal care over weeks and months, if the need is not urgent, to help clients afford services. Build out a tool kit in advance of need and advertise the availability of financing options to your clients. Veterinary practices should also recommend that owners get pet insurance and get it early in the pet's life before any preexisting conditions happen.

Still, another part of the money conversation is making sure we are using terminology that the client understands and showing the benefit to the pet. People buy on emotion. *Thinking Fast and Slow* is a best-selling book written in 2011 by Nobel Prize in Economic Sciences laureate Daniel Kahneman. In the book, he describes how humans make decisions. Before this book, it was believed that people created a logical thought path to make a wise choice, weighing the pros and cons carefully before taking the leap. In truth, that is far from how humans decide things. It was revealed that people make ninety percent of their decisions—big or small—based on gut![47]

How many people do you know who own an animal they got because someone else was going to not care for it or take it to the pound? Maybe this describes you. In that moment, your gut decided "I'll take it!" even if you already had five animals. Real estate agents know this, too. When you sell a house, you are told to make it look like you don't live there. Take down all your family photos, clean the closets, stage the furniture, fill the tub with water and floating candles and set a glass of wine on the edge, and bake bread or cookies. Now, you tell me, what does bread have to do with a real estate investment? Nothing! But when we do these things, our potential buyer's fast brain thinks, "Oh, if I live here, I will have no clutter, float in a tub with candles while drinking wine, and bake bread and cookies."

In the book *The Sandler Rules: 49 Timeless Selling Principles and How to Apply Them*, David Sandler is quoted as saying, "Every prospect or client is really three different people. The child, the parent, and the adult."[48]

Let me give you an example of how this works.

The Child sees an expensive purse. She loves the way it feels and looks when she holds it. She loves the color and even the smell of the leather. But the bag is $900. Still, the Child wants the bag. The Parent says, "You are a good Child. You work hard, you don't get many extravagant things, and you deserve a reward for how wonderful you are. You can buy the bag." The Adult justifies the purchase by thinking, "Well, the quality is excellent, the color is a good neutral and will go with all the things I wear, and they will repair it if it breaks, so I will keep it forever. If I buy fifteen $100 purses that don't last, this will really save me money over my lifetime, and, besides, IT IS ON SALE!" Sound familiar?

As medical care providers, we attempt to communicate first to the Adult. We give our medical reasoning, probable outcomes, and cost estimates set out in a logical sequence for the client. Then, we step back and ask them for a decision. This is fine for routine things that they came in for because they already wanted them but not for a new service or complex medical procedure. We must change our approach.

First, we need to recognize and reach the Child. An article I read years ago discussed a study of exam-room skills. The study discovered that doctors only listened to clients tell their story for about eleven to thirteen seconds before interrupting them and taking over the conversation. The client never got to finish what they planned to say or ask. However, when they did allow the client to go on with the full account, it only took 90 to 120 seconds, and the client left feeling better about the visit. They had accomplished everything they wanted to accomplish.

When we spend time listening—actively listening—we discover the needs of the Child because the Child says, "I WANT ..." whatever it is. If we have done a good job of listening, we know what the client is concerned about. We present our medicine in a way that supports the WANT. We need to discuss the service benefit in a more emotionally driven way.

To discover the emotional place that the pet holds in the family, we must ask our client open-ended questions. I am sure you know the definition of open-ended questions and close-ended questions, but, to me, an easy "test drive" for an open-ended question is asking myself "Does the question require that they tell me a story?"

This is our fact-finding phase. We tend to think that it is all about their medical history, but it is more. One of my favorite questions is "Where does Fluffy sleep?" This is an extremely telling question about the pet's place in the home. The answer may be "in a kennel in the laundry room." That tells me that the pet is loved, but that this may be a more practical-minded owner. The answer could also be "in his bed, which is at the foot of mine." Now we are moving up in status and sleeping in the same room. But when the answer is "he takes over my bed and sleeps between me and my wife," that pet is surely family, and the attachment is great.

I have often said that the only thing that can change the attitude of a pet owner about pets is to own a really great one—one that is so special that they change the Grinch's heart of stone to a heart the size of Texas.

Our job is to listen, listen, listen ... before we talk.

We are gathering not just medical information but also emotional data. When psychiatrists begin medical school, they are trained with this lesson: the problem that the patient brings you is never the real problem. Why does this matter to us? Because clients don't like to show their vulnerability, and they want to save face. We often listen to a client's excuse and take it at face value. Delving into the situation a little deeper may reveal some other truths. Sometimes clients are unwilling to admit their lack of medical knowledge—or even basic anatomy. Some are embarrassed to reveal how much they really love the animal, so they present it as "my wife's dog."

> **The problem that the patient brings you is never the real problem.**

Have you ever had a client lie to you? Of course, you have! Physicians automatically increase the amount of alcohol their patients admit to drinking per week because they know they fudge the truth. Remember the story of the teenager and the stoned dog? Her body language was telling the story. I used to watch the TV show *House*. I loved it. House was a skeptic. He said, "It's a basic truth of the human condition that everybody lies. The only variable is about what." This is why it is important that we confirm the pieces of information our clients are feeding us. I remember well the client who told me he had only twenty dollars and then paid with a one-hundred-dollar bill.

When you don't listen to the client and you try to advance patient care for your reasons, you will not be as successful as when you approach the care from a client-benefit direction. We have to make a discovery. Why does the client care? Remember the lesson shared earlier about how people buy based on "what's in it for me?" This was recently brought home to me by my friend, Rachel. Rachel took her well-loved but elderly cat to her veterinarian to discuss end-of-life care. The vet discussed the cat's situation, which she had been treating for several months, and suggested running another diagnostic test. Rachel asked if it would change the outcome for the cat. The doctor answered, "No." "So, why would I put her through that if it will not make any difference in her life expectancy or quality of life?" she asked. The veterinarian apologized and confessed that her scientific need to know overcame her consideration for the cat and the situation and agreed that the test was not to benefit the cat, only her curiosity. Check your reasons, and make sure they are benefiting the patient … not your desire for knowledge.

Sandler rule number twenty-seven states that "you can't sell anybody anything. They have to discover they want to buy it." What would buying or not buying this service mean to them? I often used the "many of our clients find …" approach to service offerings in practice. "Mrs. Jones, I know you told me Spot has bad gas and is almost unbearable to live with. Many of our clients find that by switching to our sensitive-stomach diet, their pets are no longer having problems and life is a lot less smelly." People tend to be followers, and if it works for someone else, they are more comfortable agreeing to the purchase.

I also used this for collecting fees prior to euthanasia. CSRs in veterinary offices understand that this is an uncomfortable but necessary thing. It makes you feel like a vulture hanging over the body when you collect money after the fact. Since most people call ahead to make arrangements, we began to use the following approach on the phone. "Mrs. Smith, I know this is a difficult time, and we are here to support you. It has helped many of our clients in the past to go ahead and take care of the financials today on the phone so when you come in, you don't even have to consider this. It will just be about you and the time you have with Spot. Would you like to do that?"

> **When people are told what to do, they tend to rebel. When people discover they need what you have, they more readily accept what you offer.**

Doctors and techs worked long and hard to learn all the facts about medicine that they know and share. But any person at the front desk can tell you a story of the client who came to the front with a diagnosis of gastroenteritis and a dazed and confused look. They scratch their head and ask your receptionist to explain what that means, even though they nodded at the doctor during the entire explanation.

I have seen oversharing of information many times in my career. We love medicine and love discussing it. But our clients don't get it, and some don't really care. **Remember that the Child is the decision maker.**

When we dump complex information on a client, talking above their head, they tend to shut down because they don't want to appear ignorant to the doctor. This is more common in young associates, who tend to feel that their vast knowledge will impress the client enough to say "yes." Unfortunately, it more likely results in a "let me think about it" response, which, to the happy ears of the doctor, is a soon-to-be "yes," but in the mind of the client was a soft let-down "no." Don't dump more information than needed on a client. Keep it simple.

You can't overcome objections if you don't know what they are.

When you stay in a practice many years like I did, you develop good relationships with your clients. Most of the time, they would tell me if they had a concern. I was the No Judgement Zone. I had clients tell me that their hesitation was not the money but instead the fact that the pet was having to stay the night. Since the dog had never been away from home, the owner feared it would panic and die of a heart attack. Together, we found a solution that worked, but only because I discovered the real reason for the "no."

One year, I was asked to lecture to a group of veterinary technicians on the subject of pet dentistry. I am a big dental advocate, but I have never performed a dental procedure in my life, and I was a little nervous. I started doing some research and found an article in the *Journal of Dental Hygiene* website where, to my surprise, I found that up to eighty percent of Americans have an inordinate fear of the dentist—so much so that at least twenty percent don't go for regular visits and nine to fifteen percent avoid getting known and needed care and going altogether.[49] A light bulb went off because I know that clients transfer their fears and emotions onto their pets. If people are afraid of the dentist and they also fear anesthesia, veterinary teams have a lot to overcome to gain a "yes" for a dental cleaning.

We need to prepare a better story to overcome those intense objections. What would be powerful enough to move you to overcome your personal fear of the dentist?

Start by asking a good question. "Mrs. Smith, I understand that you are concerned about Fluffy's oral exam and cleaning. If I told you that we were looking for broken and damaged teeth, infection and pus in the gums, and cancer of the mouth, would you feel it important for us to do that?

I think it is important that we realize we need some reframing of our education to clients. People use stories to rationalize what they perceive to be going on. Our clients are sometimes deceiving themselves when they tell us false stories. They justify their poor decisions with an attack on our fees. They accuse us of only caring about money. Keep your cool ... it is only the Child fighting with the Parent.

Review what story you are telling yourself. Analyze your feelings. What story is the client telling themselves? Diagnose the situation and act accordingly. In the words of Steven Covey, "Seek first to understand, then to be understood."[50] We have two ears and one mouth for a reason. Listen more than you talk. Answer questions with simple answers then ask more questions to confirm understanding. **Lead your clients to discover why your patient care solves a problem.** Control your own negative emotions.

We must be better at this. Our patients' well-being depends on it.

> **EXERCISE:** What reasons have clients given you to refuse your offered services? What language could you change to better overcome this objection?

16

Partnership and Collaboration: Meet Your Clients Where They Are

Hospitality requires that we shape our systems to accommodate the wishes and needs of our clients. When practices don't invest in modern technology tools that allow their clients to communicate easily with the practice, they are intentionally causing roadblocks to access to care.

As a frequent traveler, I can say that without my hotel, rental car, and airline apps, I would not only be inconvenienced but also aggravated if I had to attempt to book rooms, cars, or flights with a phone call. With a few clicks of a mouse, I can look at my accommodations, find a car that suits my needs, and compare flights. Recently, I visited a veterinary hospital with my new dog, Tucker. I called to make his appointment and had a nice customer service experience. I received an email notifying me to download the vet hospital's app, which I did. A few weeks later, I received a voicemail reminding me of Tucker's appointment and noting that, to confirm this event, I had to call the practice, which I did. Upon entering the clinic, I was given a clipboard with new patient and client paperwork to complete and then was called back to visit the doctor. Tucker had his visit, and there was some poor communication, so when I rated the practice, I gave it an average review. The practice manager called me to discuss my rating and my experience. I explained that I was a little irritated that I couldn't confirm my appointment online and that I didn't have the option of completing my new client paperwork digitally. I felt that this was an indication that the practice was behind the times. Of course, I eventually found out that I could have performed both functions in the app, but the person who called me never offered that option. She had been saying "call us to confirm" for so many years that she didn't change her spiel to include "or confirm in the app." The point of the story is that if you plan to offer the latest conveniences to your clients, make sure you tell clients that you have them.

> **If you plan to offer the latest conveniences to your clients, make sure you tell clients that you have them.**

Technology tools are a double-edged sword. In one aspect, they can save teams a lot of time by automating tasks and processes that humans used to do, freeing up many minutes or even hours in a day. On the opposite side, they can make communication impersonal. If we plan to take advantage of automation, we should use the valuable time we gain to connect on a human level with our clients. We should never lose sight of the importance of building relationships with others.

That being said, there are many studies that show that younger generations desire to use digital tools to make their own appointments, confirm those appointments, send text messages to the team or doctor, receive text messages on health status, fill out forms, view diagnostic results, share immunization history with other providers, request medication refills, and even use telehealth to triage health issues with themselves or their pet before heading to the ER. To serve this tech savvy generation well, we must embrace technology. However, we must never exclude older generations who do not live in a digital world. We must not ignore or discount them; rather, we should make sure our communication efforts cover all the avenues necessary to serve our clients well.

> **Practices cannot assume that everyone they care for is online.**

Seniors make up a large segment of our database. All must be considered when we are sending out important information such as reminders for services, medication and product recalls, and health alerts about contagious diseases.

Technology tools give practices the opportunity to educate people about health conditions so they can be informed about how to help themselves or their pets. Many studies share that when people receive written information in a language they can understand, which supports the instructions or education they receive from their provider, they are more likely to follow-through on care. People in exam rooms are often distracted and upset. Sharing information they can reference later helps them remember their instructions.

Many years ago, my practice took the time to create written take-home instructions for almost every procedure we performed. The documents were tied to service codes, and when the invoices were printed out for the client, the instructions were automatically printed, too. In today's world, we can attach web links to video instructions showing how to administer medications. This would certainly save time for the team because clients often go home and then call back to get the directions again because they either forgot or were not a hundred percent comfortable with what they remembered.

Successful providers are forward thinkers. Using tech to connect is a great way to save time while still providing personalized service.

> **EXERCISE:** Consider the technology that you have in your practice. How can you improve service to your clients through this tool? What gaps in service need to be filled?

Conclusion

Proof That Hospitality Works in Healthcare

Let's face it—providing great hospitality to clients requires effort. The question is, is it worth it? A recent Harvard Business Review article titled "When Patient Experience and Employee Engagement Both Improve, Hospitals' Ratings and Profits Climb" found a distinct correlation between patient satisfaction scores and employee engagement, where high marks in both translated to a direct increase in profits.[51] In another article, "How U.S. Health Care Got Safer by Focusing on the Patient Experience," the authors shared the following: "My colleagues and I have analyzed data on patient experience as well as publicly reported data on patient safety and business performance. We have found that these performance 'outcomes' are correlated—that is, the organizations with better patient experience also have better safety records and report better financial margins."[52] These are just a couple of the many articles and data points that show that improving culture and creating a great patient experience in a medical facility can result in a happier team, happier consumers, and higher profits.

If we want to solve the many issues in medicine, we must move towards a hospitality mindset—not just for our patients but also with our coworkers. Collaboration, as humans evolved to do, is the path toward better job satisfaction. When teams work together with a common goal, in kindness and harmony, they can accomplish great feats of healing. Leaders must realize that dictatorial orders from above and driving medical professionals for profit alone only demotivates and causes anguish in their subordinates. Instead of working to create a positive culture and outstanding client experience, employees who have leaders that are harsh and uncaring have to mentally "gird their loins" just to walk in the door. They keep their heads down and hope for the best. It is no wonder that they are leaving the profession in droves.[53] However, if practices can embrace the rules of true hospitality and care for their clients and their team members as the valuable and important people that they are, they can see high employee retention, extraordinary client satisfaction, and a bottom line that is the envy of their competitors.

> **Great hospitality can create a practice that everyone wants to come to, everyone wants to work at, and everyone wants to buy.**

Humans are born to help each other. It is how we survived for eons and how we thrive today. Our brains are wired to experience joy when we give joy to others. I once listened to a keynote address by Michael J. Fox at a veterinary conference. It just so happened that because of his advanced Parkinson's disease, he had stumbled up the stage steps. He righted himself and made his way to the podium where I noticed his hands were scraped and bleeding. He never wavered but instead gave his speech. I will always remember when he said, "If you ever feel bad or sorry for yourself, go do something for someone else. I guarantee you will feel better!" He is right.

So, I challenge you to work to change the world around you for the better by using the lessons from this book. Each of us has the opportunity to share random acts of kindness many times a day. We need to make a point to do so. If we do, our work and homes will be more enjoyable places to be. Always assume positive intent and give grace to others. Then, watch the positive results roll in.

Appendices

Exam Room – Time and Motion Study

The idea behind the Time and Motion Study is to track, with accuracy, the actual time it takes to work with a client and patient, from the time they enter the practice until checkout. It is only when we measure that we truly know how to efficiently use our appointment schedule to its maximum benefit.

It will be easier to calculate the times if you use military hours, e.g., 2:00 p.m. is 14:00 hours. You may choose to highlight the species in different colors of highlighter to easily sort them at the end of the day.

This will be a team effort. Check after each other to confirm you have tracked the times. Do the calculations frequently and during downtime or it will be too overwhelming. Track for at least two weeks to give a good, well-rounded view of "normal" time frames. There will always be the surprise chatty client, but we are seeking averages.

> **TIP:** You may want to invest in some inexpensive clip-on timers for your rooms. These can act as a stopwatch in case you lose track of the time on the clock.

At the end of the testing and tracking period, sort the study cards into species and "type" of appointment. You may also sort them again by provider to see if certain doctors are faster or slower than others. The appointment book is a tool that can be sharply tuned with the right information.

EXAM ROOM – TIME AND MOTION STUDY

Date _____

Customer care representative _____

Species: CA   FE   Other _____

If sick, describe illness: _____

_____

_____

DVM _____   Tech _____

Appointment time _____

Arrival time _____   Time into room _____

DVM time into room _____   DVM time out _____

Tech time into room _____   Tech time out _____

CSR time of checkout _____

Type of visit (check one):

☐ Annual Vax

☐ Pup/Kit 1st

☐ Pup/Kit Series

☐ Senior Annual

☐ Sick Patient

☐ Behavior

☐ Derm

☐ Medical Discharge

☐ Oral Exam

☐ Nutrition

☐ Anal Exp

☐ Nail Trim (Normal)

☐ Nail Trim (Difficult)

Total wait time to get in room

Total time in room

Onboarding Plan

Here is a three-phase plan developed for onboarding new team members.

PHASE I

After Hiring and Before Start Date

1. If an employee has to relocate to your area, assist the new hire with information about the area. You might send articles of interest from the local newspaper—especially if clients are mentioned. This will give the new employee a grounding in the local market.

2. Refer the employee to a local real estate agent—preferably a client—to assist in housing procurement.

3. Provide a list of good schools, areas of town to avoid that have high crime rates, good restaurants for both dine-in and delivery, reputable auto repair shops, and the locations of local grocery stores.

4. Discover their hobbies and assist them in locating suppliers or locations to pursue them (for example, a runner needs a safe running track to use).

5. Find out if they have children. Can you recommend safe day-care centers or babysitters?

For Everyone Hired

6. Send a list of staff member names, staff positions and experience levels, and other relevant information on "day one" so that the new employee can recognize at least some of the names. This will make your new employee feel as if they know someone other than their interviewer and also shows your staff members that they are important as team members. Adding photographs is even better.

7. Have uniforms or lab coats ordered and ready for day one and have business cards and name tags ready if appropriate.

8. Mail a copy of the job description to allow it to be read thoroughly and learned before the first day on the job.

9. Mail a copy of the floor plan (especially if it's a larger facility) so the new team member may orient themselves to the building.

10. Have a workspace prepared. For example, if the new employee needs a desk, have it ready and in place before they come to work.

11. Choose a trainer and discuss with them their duties in training the new employee. Make sure that the trainer is a person you would like your new employee to emulate and that they have both the interest and the social skills to do the job.

12. Choose a mentor. The duty of the mentor is to help the new person understand the dynamics of the people in the practice. They are different from the trainer because they are the go-to person if there is a problem with the trainer or other staff members. They are there to help the person assimilate into the culture.

13. "Presell" your new employee to the clients and the staff. This is especially important for new veterinarians or physicians who often have problems getting established clients to work with them. Tout their skills, education, special interests, and experience to all that will listen.

PHASE II

First Day

1. Day one should be a celebration. Invite the family of the new employee to visit and meet coworkers.

2. Place a banner in the lobby introducing and welcoming your new hire.

3. Introduce them to their mentor and trainer.

4. Make sure the mentor is free to greet the new employee and introduce them to all the staff.

5. Give the employee an orientation tour of the hospital. Show them their work area, office, or desk.

6. Allow the employee time to fill out all standard tax forms, give them a copy of the employee manual, and have them sign that they received it. Have them sign all internal policies and store them in their employee file. Verify and record identification information. Complete all paperwork pertaining to benefits. Confirm with the employee their understanding of important policies: benefits, payroll information, vacation policy, etc.

7. Have the mentor explain the history of the practice, any partnerships or sister practices, if appropriate, and the dynamic of the group.

8. Give the employee the list of common questions (provided in the next section).

9. Explain the pattern of the flow of work.

10. Review goals for the day. For example, a new doctor will review all drugs in the pharmacy to familiarize herself with resources, or a new technician will shadow an experienced technician to learn exam-room procedures for a vaccination visit.

11. Show the location of safety equipment (e.g., fire extinguishers, eye-wash stations, protective clothing, etc.).

12. Set goals for the week. For example, a new office manager will interview all employees and discuss job descriptions.

13. Plan time for the end of week one to review the week, confirm that goals were met, and confirm with the employee that the trainer and mentor are providing them with education and feedback in a constructive manner.

PHASE III

1. Set longer-term goals, weekly and then monthly, for new employees.

2. Plan time to review goals and results with the employee, offering suggestions for improvement or encouragement for progress.

3. Create an action plan for advanced training, with timelines and reviews.

4. Reiterate the goals of the practice and confirm that the new hire understands the practice goals, mission, and core values.

5. Ask for feedback from the employee on company protocols. Remember that a fresh set of eyes often reveals areas needing improvement.

Common Questions We Should Answer for Our New Hires

- What is my schedule?
- Who is my supervisor?
- What do I wear?
- Where do I park?
- Where is the restroom?
- Where is the break room?
- Where are the office supplies? Who do I ask if I need something?
- Who orders medical supplies?

- Who orders office supplies?

- Where do soiled towels go?

- Where are fresh towels and blankets stored?

- What is the internet policy?

- What is my email address?

- What is the mailing address of the hospital?

- What are the telephone numbers?

- How does the intercom work?

- How does the phone system work?

- How do I retrieve voicemail messages?

- What diets do we recommend?

- What parasite preventatives do we recommend?

- What are our vaccination protocols?

- What are our requirements for pre-anesthetic lab work?

- Where do we send "outside" lab samples?

- What is our computer software system, and how can I learn the program?

- Who handles "upset" clients?

- When will I get my first paycheck?

- Who do I speak to if I have a problem with a fellow worker?

- How do I get continuing education?

- When do we have meetings, and are they mandatory?

- What is the procedure for bringing my pet to be treated?

- What is the payment policy for employees' animals?

- When am I allowed breaks?

- When am I allowed to make personal phone calls?

- What is the employee warning and discharge policy?

- Where are the required Department of Labor posters posted?

- How do I record my time?

- What do I do if I make a mistake on my timecard?

- What do I do if I break or spill a controlled drug?

- Where do I record controlled drugs?

- Who do I tell if equipment is broken?

- Who do I tell if I witness an employee stealing?

- What do I do if I see my supervisor or the owner make a mistake?

- What do I do if a patient "has an accident" on the floor?

- What do I do if I suspect that a patient is contagious?

- What do I do if there is an aggressive animal in the lobby?

- Who do I tell if there is a problem with the practice facility, e.g., a stopped-up toilet?

- What is the procedure for an emergency?

- What is the procedure for a fire in the building?

- What is the protocol for a sick animal whose owner has no funds?

- What is our credit card policy, and what types of payment to we accept?

- Who repairs computer problems?

- What is our procedure for patient euthanasia?

- What are our requirements for medication refills?

- Who will review my job performance, and when will my first review be given?

- What are common medical problems specific to our area?

- What unique services do we offer our patients?

- What unique services do our competitors offer their patients that we don't?

- What medical problems do we refer to specialty hospitals?

- Do any members of our staff have special skills that can be marketed to clients?

- What products do we sell for dental care?

- Who are our "frequent flyer" clients?

- What species of animals do we treat?

- How many times do we walk boarding dogs per day?

- What do we feed boarding animals?

- Do any employees have issues, medical challenges, allergies, or problems that I should be aware of? (Make sure to not disclose medical history, but you don't want the new hire to accidentally make an inappropriate remark because they don't know something that everyone else knows.)

This list is certainly not every question that a new team member will need to know, and, yes, some of them should be answered in the employee manual, provided that it is up to date. All practices are different, and you are advised to add questions to the list for future use. Still, this list will certainly help a new person orient themselves to the practice and help them avoid awkward and potentially embarrassing situations.

The Steps of Successful Delegation

1. Look at the task itself. Is it something that can be delegated?

2. Choose the staff member to perform the task, checking to see if they have the knowledge, skills, and interest in the task. Will they learn from the task? Will you gain from the delegation?

3. Will you give them, or do they have, the tools needed to perform the task? Do they understand what to do? Will you need to do some training?

4. Tell them why this task is important, necessary, and useful.

5. What is the desired end result? Don't assume that they know. How will you measure or determine completion?

6. Discuss what resources will be needed.

7. Both the manager and staff members must agree to the timeline. For ongoing tasks, when will management review progress? Deadlines are important.

8. Share the delegation with the rest of the team so they can support their coworker as well as understand why this person's job duties have changed.

9. Give feedback! Give credit! Don't abandon them if the task did not go as planned. Use the failure as a training lesson.

Finally, be kind. Team members have a great desire to feel SAFE in their work and home environments. When they are demeaned or threatened with job loss, they can't perform to the best of their abilities.

Core Values

Use this list as a foundation for creating your own facility's core values.

Performance – Our team will manifest outstanding performance by always following through on our work. When we see a job to be done, we will step up and complete it. To support great performance, we will work to show appreciation to one another for work well done.

Adaptable – Veterinary medicine is often unpredictable and ever changing. To serve our clients and patients, we will gladly learn new skills and share our skills with one another. We will help one another when faced with difficult patients or clients by offering to trade off. We will also agree to "laugh more and cry less" when our days throw us curveballs, always reacting with humor rather than drama.

Professional – We will work on self-mastery by controlling our minds and emotions and not allowing others to draw us to a negative place. We will always be willing to ask questions and disclose when we don't know an answer. We will maintain a professional image that is caring, nonjudgmental, and empathetic. We will act to read others' emotional states and communicate in an appropriate manner to help them.

Informative – We recognize that we are teachers and that our job is to educate our clients by meeting them at their knowledge level. We will also assume positive intent in our interactions with others.

Efficient – In order to maximize our efficiency, we recognize that our environment must remain neat, clean, and well organized, and we are committed to sustaining high standards in these areas. Standard operating procedures will be created and followed. Lists will be built to keep us from missing important duties, and labels will be used so that every item has its place. By doing so, we can serve our patients, their owners, and one another in the most timely manner.

Integrity – We agree that our greatest asset is our personal integrity. Because of this, we will always be open to giving and receiving feedback without taking offense. Our behavior will be respectful, honest, and ethical. We will only recommend care that is needed for our patients, and we will find a way to care for patients in crisis if at all possible. We will be on time for work and will make our best effort while working, as this shows respect for our employer and for one another.

By agreeing to live these core values, we will create and maintain a culture of joy, trust, and kindness. Our practice will be successful because of the exceptional care that we offer our clients and patients. Our team will enjoy a work environment that is the envy of other hospitals, and we will be known as a practice of excellence in our community.

Welcome Letter Example

Use this letter as a foundation for creating your own personalized letter that's sent from your practice to your new patients.

Dear [title] [first name] [last name],

The staff of The Animal Hospital would like to take a moment to thank you for choosing our hospital for your pet's care. We feel privileged to be able to provide veterinary and pet resort services for [animal's name]. Our goal is to offer superior medical care at a great value, an immaculate state-of-the-art facility for our patients' and clients' comfort, and exceptional customer service.

Our hours are Monday from 7:00 a.m. to 8:00 p.m.; Tuesday, Wednesday, and Thursday from 7:00 a.m. to 7:00 p.m.; Friday from 7:00 a.m. to 6:00 p.m.; and Saturday from 8:00 a.m. to 2:00 p.m. Please visit our website at [web address] to learn more about our team and visit our online pharmacy. We are happy to offer in-home delivery for all your pet's needs. Our Pet Resort & Spa also offers a medically supervised, full-service boarding facility with playtime, day care, and luxury suites furnished with webcams, TVs, and luxury bedding, along with spa services for the truly spoiled pet.

We have an outstanding and dedicated team of doctors, pet nurses, client care representatives, and resort staff to help partner with you to take the best possible care of your animal family member. We offer many advanced medical services, including an extensive array of surgical procedures, dentistry with digital radiology, hospitalization, and wellness care. Our facility is equipped with digital radiology, a complete in-house diagnostic laboratory, blood-pressure monitoring, ultrasound, a video otoscope, a laser surgery unit, and glaucoma screening. All this means that we can get results rapidly and treat patients without waiting when time is of the essence. We know that clients want to take great care of their pets, so client education and communication is a top priority.

Our doctors are focused on keeping your pet healthy. In keeping with the American Veterinary Medical Association and American Animal Hospital Association guidelines, we recommend a nose-to-tail physical examination twice a year. Pets age at a much faster rate than people, so a visit every six months is the equivalent of a child visiting their doctor every three years! Many times, with thorough physical exams and screening blood work, pets can be saved from months of unnecessary illness and suffering. Often, problems can be resolved with a simple change in diet.

We know that quality veterinary care is what our clients want for their pets, but costs can be challenging; so we offer multiple payment options which include all major credit cards (Visa, MasterCard, American Express, and Discover) and CareCredit®, a health and pet care credit card. Clients can apply for CareCredit® in our office, online at www. carecredit.com/apply, or by calling 1-866-893-7864. CareCredit® offers promotional financing options on purchases of $200 or more. We also strongly encourage you to investigate and purchase pet insurance as a safety net for the unexpected issues that often arise.

Once again, we thank you for allowing us to care for your pets. Please do not hesitate to call our office with questions or suggestions. We look forward to serving you and your animal family members for many years to come.

Sincerely,

The Doctors and Staff of The Animal Hospital

Notes

1   John Medina, "The Proust Effect" in *Brain Rules*, 212-214.

2   John Medina, "Principles for Surviving and Thriving at Work, Home, and School" in *Brain Rules,* 12, 84-87.

3   Daphne Maurer and Philip Salapatek, "Developmental Changes in the Scanning of Faces by Young Infants," *Child Development*, June 1976, vol. 47, no. 2, 523-527.

4   "Be Prepared for an Active Shooter," Federal Emergency Management Agency website, accessed May 2, 2023, https://community.fema.gov/ProtectiveActions/s/article/Active-Shooter.

5   Paul Ekman, "Facial Expressions" in Tim Dalgleish and Mick J. Power (eds.), *Handbook of Cognition and Emotion,* 301-320.

6   "Even Small Distractions Derail Productivity," Association for Psychological Science website, accessed May 2, 2023, https://www.psychologicalscience.org/news/minds-business/even-small-distractions-derail-productivity.html.

7   Veterinary Social Work Resource List, accessed May 2, 2023, http://vetsocialwork.utk.edu/wp-content/uploads/2018/04/Pet-Loss-Resource-Listupdated-April-2018-.pdf.

8   The Lifeline and 988, 988 Suicide & Crisis Hotline website, accessed May 2, 2023, https://988lifeline.org/current-events/the-lifeline-and-988.

9   Suicide Prevention and Mental Health seminar offering, American Veterinary Medical Association website, accessed May 2, 2023, https://axon.avma.org/local/catalog/view/product.php?productid=148.

10 Suicide Prevention Guide to Treat At-Risk Patients, American Medical Association website, accessed May 2, 2023, https://www.ama-assn.org/delivering-care/public-health/suicide-prevention-guide-treat-risk-patients.

11 Animal Charities & Helpful Financing Ideas for Pet Owners with Sick Pets, Debbie Boone website, accessed May 2, 2023, https://debbieboonecvpm.com/help-for-pet-owners.

12 Cynthia L. Ogden, Ph.D.; Cheryl D. Fryar, M.S.P.H.; Margaret D. Carroll, M.S.P.H.; and Katherine M. Flegal, Ph.D., "Mean Body Weight, Height, and Body Mass Index, United States 1960-2002," Division of Health and Nutrition Examination Surveys, U.S. Department of Health and Human Services, Centers for Disease Control and Prevention, accessed May 2, 2023, https://www.cdc.gov/nchs/data/ad/ad347.pdf.

13 Erik Lindecrantz, Madeleine Tjon, Pian Gi, and Stefano Zerbi, "Personalizing the Customer Experience: Driving Differentiation in Retail," McKinsey & Company website, accessed May 2, 2023, https://www.mckinsey.com/industries/retail/our-insights/personalizing-the-customer-experience-driving-differentiation-in-retail.

14 Will Guadara, "The Secret Ingredients of Great Hospitality," TED Talk, accessed May 2, 2023, https://www.ted.com/talks/will_guidara_the_secret_ingredients_of_great_hospitality.

15 Dealing With Difficult People. Pryor Training, accessed May 2, 2023, https://www.pryor.com/training-seminars/dealing-with-difficult-people.

16 Color Personality Test, accessed May 2, 2023, https://www.colorpersonalitytest.org.

17	The Myers-Briggs Foundation, accessed May 2, 2023, https://www.myersbriggs.org.

18	The Enneagram Institute, accessed May 2, 2023, https://www.enneagraminstitute.com.

19	Theodore B. Kinni, *Be Our Guest: Perfecting the Art of Customer Service,* (New York: Disney Editions, 2001).

20	Core Values List, James Clear website, accessed May 2, 2023, https://jamesclear.com/core-values.

21	Tom Wujec, "Got a Wicked Problem? First, Tell Me How You Make Toast," TED Talk, accessed June 2, 2023, https://www.ted.com/talks/tom_wujec_got_a_wicked_problem_first_tell_me_how_you_make_toast

22	Sophia Yin, *Low Stress Handling Restraint and Behavior Modification of Dogs & Cats: Techniques for Developing Patients Who Love Their Visits*, (Davis, CA, CattleDog Publishing, 2009).

23	Fear Free® website, accessed May 2, 2023, https://fearfreepets.com.

24	Iatrophobia (Fear of Doctors), Cleveland Clinic website, accessed May 2, 2023, https://my.clevelandclinic.org/health/diseases/22191-iatrophobia-fear-of-doctors.

25	Food Insecurity in the US, Key Statistics & Graphs, United States Department of Agriculture website, accessed May 2, 2023, https://www.ers.usda.gov/topics/food-nutrition-assistance/food-security-in-the-u-s/key-statistics-graphics/#insecure.

26	Biases in Healthcare: An Overview, *Medical News Today*, accessed May 2, 2023, https://www.medicalnewstoday.com/articles/biases-in-healthcare.

27	Project Implicit, accessed May 2, 2023, https://implicit.harvard.edu/implicit/education.html.

28	Janice A. Sabin, PhD, MSW, "Tackling Implicit Bias in Health Care" in *The New England Journal of Medicine,* July 14, 2022, vol. 387, 105-107, accessed May 2, 2023, https://www.nejm.org/doi/full/10.1056/NEJMp2201180.

29	FitzGerald, Chloë and Samia Hurst, "Implicit Bias in Healthcare Professionals: A Systematic Review," *BMC Medical Ethics,* March 1, 2017, vol. 18, no. 19, accessed May 2, 2023, https://bmcmedethics.biomedcentral.com/articles/10.1186/s12910-017-0179-8.

30	Janice A. Sabin, PhD, MSW, "Tackling Implicit Bias in Health Care" in *The New England Journal of Medicine,* July 14, 2022, vol. 387, 105-107, accessed May 2, 2023, https://www.nejm.org/doi/full/10.1056/NEJMp2201180.

31	Sai Balasubramaniam, MD, JD. August 26, 2022, "The Healthcare Industry is Crumbling Due to Staffing Shortages" in *Forbes*, accessed May 2, 2023, https://www.forbes.com/sites/saibala/2022/08/26/the-healthcare-industry-is-crumbling-due-to-staffing-shortages.

32	Tasha Eurich, *Insight: The Surprising Truth About How Others See Us, How We See Ourselves, and Why the Answers Matter More Than We Think*, (New York: Currency Penguin Random House, 2018).

33	Christine Pearson and Christine Porath, *The Cost of Bad Behavior: How Incivility Is Damaging Your Business and What to Do About It*, (New York: Portfolio Penguin Random House, 2009).

34	Pearson and Porath, *The Cost of Bad Behavior*, 1-2.

35	Pearson and Porath, *The Cost of Bad Behavior*.

36   Roy Mauer. March 3, 2015, "FBI: Over 80 Percent of Active Shooter Incidents Occur at Work,"
      Society for Human Resource Management website, accessed May 2, 2023, https://www.shrm.org/
      ResourcesAndTools/hr-topics/risk-management/Pages/FBI-Active-Shooter-Work.aspx.

37   Travis Bradberry and Jean Greaves, *Emotional Intelligence 2.0,* (San Diego, CA: TalentSmart, 2009).

38   John Medina, *Brain Rules: 12 Principles for Surviving and Thriving at Work, Home and School*, (Seattle:
      Pear Press, 2008), 40-42.

39   John Medina, *Brain Rules*, 183-188.

40   Christine Pearson and Christine Porath, 2009, *The Cost of Bad Behavior: How Incivility Is Damaging
      Your Business and What to Do About It*, New York: Portfolio (Penguin Random House), 73.

41   Emma Seppälä and Kim Cameron, December 1, 2015, "Proof That Positive Work Cultures are More
      Productive" in *Harvard Business Review,* accessed May 2, 2023, https://hbr.org/2015/12/proof-that-
      positive-work-cultures-are-more-productive.

42   Joseph Greeny, Ron McMillan, Al Switzler, Kerry Patterson, and Laura Roppe, *Crucial Conversations:
      Tools for Talking When Stakes Are High*, (New York: McGraw Hill, 2002).

43   Travis Bradberry and Jean Greaves, *Emotional Intelligence 2.0,* (San Diego, CA: TalentSmart, 2009).

44   The Gottman Institute, accessed May 2, 2023, https://www.gottman.com.

45   Lifetime of Care Study, Synchrony, accessed May 2, 2023, http://petlifetimeofcare.com.

46   VHMA Strategic Pricing Pet Owner Economic Value Study, Veterinary Hospital Managers Association
      website, accessed May 2, 2023, https://members.vhma.org/store/ViewProduct.aspx?id=14901966.

47   Daniel Kahneman, *Thinking Fast and Slow,* (New York: Farrar, Straus, and Giroux, 2013).

48   David Mattson, *The Sandler Rules: 49 Timeless Selling Principles and How to Apply Them,*
      (Beverly Hills, CA: Pegasus Media World, 2009).

49   Angela M. White, Lori Giblin, and Linda D. Boyd, February 2017, "The Prevalence of Dental Anxiety in
      Dental Practice Settings" in American Dental Hygienists' Association's *Journal of Dental Hygiene,* vol.
      91, no. 1, 30-34.

50   Stephen Covey, *The 7 Habits of Highly Effective People: Powerful Lessons in Personal Change*,
      (New York: Simon & Schuster, 1989).

51   Nell W. Buhlman and Thomas H. Lee, May 8, 2019, "When Patient Experience and Employee
      Engagement Both Improve, Hospitals' Ratings and Profits Climb" in *Harvard Business Review,* accessed
      May 2, 2023, https://hbr.org/2019/05/when-patient-experience-and-employee-engagement-both-
      improve-hospitals-ratings-and-profits-climb.

52   Thomas H. Lee, May 31, 2017, "How U.S. Health Care Got Safer by Focusing on the Patient Experience,"
      in *Harvard Business Review,* accessed May 2, 2023, https://hbr.org/2017/05/how-u-s-health-care-got-
      safer-by-focusing-on-the-patient-experience.

53   Ed Yong, November 16, 2021, "Why Health-Care Workers are Quitting in Droves," in *The Atlantic,*
      accessed May 2, 2023, https://www.theatlantic.com/health/archive/2021/11/the-mass-exodus-of-
      americas-health-care-workers/620713.

www.ingramcontent.com/pod-product-compliance
Lightning Source LLC
Chambersburg PA
CBHW031403180326
41458CB00043B/6587/J

* 9 7 8 1 9 5 3 3 1 5 3 0 4 *